LIFE
A Celebration

Kartar Singh is the Chairman Emeritus of Amber Group. His earlier book, *Dhyan: Superpower of Man*, received much acclaim.

LIFE

A Celebration

KARTAR SINGH

RUPA

Published by
Rupa Publications India Pvt. Ltd 2023
7/16, Ansari Road, Daryaganj
New Delhi 110002

Sales Centres:

Prayagraj Bengaluru Chennai
Hyderabad Jaipur Kathmandu
Kolkata Mumbai

P-ISBN: 978-93-5702-476-1
E-ISBN: 978-93-5702-473-0

First impression 2023

10 9 8 7 6 5 4 3 2 1

The moral right of the author has been asserted.

Printed in India

CONTENTS

v

PART-2
EXPERIENCE LIFE BEYOND SPACE AND TIME

PART-3
LIFE: A CELEBRATION

INTRODUCTION

People in this world are constantly chasing happiness. They are too ignorant to realize that the chase itself is the source of their sorrow. They can never be happy if they keep wasting their precious energy, which is the ultimate source of happiness.

Regardless of one's status, appearance or education, true happiness is only attainable once a person has cultivated a high level of awareness. A beggar who has cultivated a high level of awareness may experience more genuine happiness than a king who lacks that quality. The level of one's awareness is the only true measure of happiness.

This book will awaken readers to the ways they may have been moving in the wrong direction and losing their most precious energy: the energy of the self. It will empower readers to transform their lives and regain their lost energy to achieve true happiness.

Lack of clarity about things and situations can cause people to suffer and lead them towards a bleak path. The energy of the self or awareness can be a guiding light. As people become more aware, they experience greater clarity, leading to the path of happiness.

PART-1

HUMAN AWAKENING
FOR ETERNAL BLISS

1

FALL FROM GRACE

Babies undergo a complex developmental process when still inside the womb of their mothers. But the beginning of life is considered to be the moment at which they exit the womb and come into the real world. It is when they are delivered and separated from the mother that they take their first breath on their own, marking the beginning of life. This momentous occasion is called 'birth'. When they are born, children possess no prior knowledge or experience; they are pure souls. However, they possess an enormous amount of energy; energy that is connected to the self, which I am going to be referring to as the 'energy of the self' throughout this book. This energy enables them to be observant and witness everything happening in their surroundings. Children exude an incredible amount of positive energy, which makes them highly active, full of life, and curious about the world. During the early stages of life, children's minds are not yet developed, which allows them to remain focussed and unburdened by distracting thoughts.

Initially, infants observe the world without any judgement or feeling of attachment. They lack the cognitive development necessary to form opinions or fully comprehend the experience of birth, life or death. At this stage, they are merely a 'witness', disconnected from the physical world around them but connected to the universe as a whole. Their true nature, characterized by freedom and eternal bliss, is evident.

One of the first motor skills that children develop is feeding on their mother's milk. The more milk the children have, the more they desire it and soon begin experiencing feelings of hunger. This feeling is a small step in unlocking the infinite consciousness that allows the child's mind to develop. As children begin to grow, they experience many things, including the feeling of hunger, the comfort in the touch of their mother, the expulsion of waste and sensations of other bodily functions. These experiences create subtle movements in their consciousness, which continue to build the foundation of their developing mind. As children move from being mere observers to active participants in their surroundings, they also begin retaining information and unlock the power of memory. Memories form the foundation for their thinking process since it is through memories,

When children are fed their mother's milk, they do not fully understand what it is, yet the experience initiates a sense of feeling. With this initiation of feeling starts the formation of the 'mind'.

experiences and perceptions that their intellect is developed. A child's mind, unlike an adult's, is mostly devoid of any judgements.

As children's minds develop further, their ability to percieve the world around them and retain information strengthens… However, their reasoning skills have not yet developed. Their understanding of the world is still very limited, owing to their underdeveloped minds. Children start responding to the name given to them, but they do not fully understand the concept of identity, they just respond out of habit. This marks the initial stages of the formation of the self or 'I'. However, children may incorrectly start using phrases like 'I am' or 'mine' to refer to their body or possessions because they assume that this is what the self is.

This is a natural development in the lives of humans and leads to the strengthening of their **ego**. The ego is something that corrupts the inherent innocence of children. Children soon fall prey to the materialistic nature of the real world, without realizing the misery that lies beyond it. This ego, if the children let it consume them, can take control of their lives, and lead them away from their inherent pure consciousness.

Associating the "I" with the self means letting the ego take control. The ego is infectious, almost like a virus. If this virus can be eliminated from children's lives, they will be able to live in harmony and with a sense of oneness with the universe. They will experience total freedom and eternal bliss.

The mind develops according to the child's perceptions of its surroundings. The mind is nothing but a consequence of the feelings and observations of the world around, and of one's own body. If the child is able to control these feelings and develop a sense of calmness, it can lead to the development of a universal mind, devoid of ego and detached from the self.

Education is crucial to a child's development. Children need to be taught how to maintain their relationship with the spiritual world. Without education, children would lead ignorant lives controlled by their ego.

Unfortunately, our current education system fails to provide children with a framework for understanding their true nature. Instead, it focusses solely on teaching them how to survive in the material world, neglecting spiritual knowledge.

If children were to receive proper education about the self and their true nature, formal education will become easy for them. Children who are full of the energy of the self can effortlessly do whatever they set their mind to. Such children will lead society into an era of peace and harmony.

In the absence of proper spiritual education, children are becoming increasingly trapped in their ego, losing touch with the energy of the self. This is cultivating negative energy and making them lead miserable lives. Children are meant to radiate postive energy, and the lack of spiritual education is causing them to spread negativity in society. As each new child is born, the whole society and the world at large experiences a further depletion of positive energy, resulting in greater suffering.

2

THE NATURE OF THE MIND

Human emotions, feelings and thoughts serve as the building blocks of perception, and their constant movement within the consciousness is what gives birth to the concept of the "mind."

In Vedanta philosophy, the 'mind' is said to have four functions:

1. Deliberation
2. Memory
3. Determination
4. Ego

Every time we percive something in this world, our mind undergoes these four steps in rapid succession, making them seem like one.

Let's consider an example to illustrate how the four

functions of the mind operate in creating our perceptions. Suppose you see a potted plant. Your first reaction is to wonder what it is, which corresponds to the function of deliberation. Then you attempt to recollect if you have seen it before, which utilizes the function of memory. Once you recognize the plant, your intellect determines and confirms that it is indeed a potted plant, reflecting the function of determination. Upon recognition, you experience a feeling of pride at your ability to identify the object, which reflects the function of the ego.

The mind is an important tool for navigating the material world, but it often functions automatically without our active involvement. As we become adults and take on responsibilities—such as work, marriage, children etc.—our attention gets divided among various stimuli: our job, family, social circles, electronic devices, and more. This constant overload can leave us feeling restless and drained, with little control over our thoughts and emotions. Our racing mind can use up all the energy of the self, leaving us miserable. We lose self-control when the energy of the self is low, increasing our woes. We need to understand the nature of the mind to resolve this problem.

Sant Kabir wrote: *Rasree avat jaat se sill per parat nisan.* (If a rope moves up and down and rubs against a stone, it leaves its impression on it.) In the past, people used to fetch water from deep wells using a bucket tied to a rope. To lift the filled bucket, they would pull it over a stone placed at the edge of the well. As the rope was repeatedly pulled and

The 'mind' can be described as waves in the ocean of the self.

released, it would cut deeper and deeper into the stone. The constant movement would ultimately create a groove. The rope would slip automatically into the groove even if one tried to prevent that.

Similarly, when we constantly keep running our mind, it becomes habitual. This makes its way deeper and deeper into our memory; the mind cannot stop racing. Even if someone diverts our attention for some time, the mind falls back into the same groove or habit. This ingrained behaviour can be difficult to alter. It is almost like an addiction and can be called the conditioning of the mind.

When people engage in activities with a lack of attention or low energy, the addiction or conditioning of the mind can become severe. The lack of alertness can lead to unfulfilment in life, and it forces people to start looking at shortcuts to success. This causes further suffering as they now rely on instant gratification instead on effortless effort, therefore reinforcing the conditioning of the mind. The lower the energy of the self, the more the mind becomes conditioned. This is why ignorant people lead miserable lives.In contrast, people with spiritual knowledge remain connected to the self and remain calm from within due to a high level of energy. They are constanly engaged in activities, and this gives them a sense of satisfaction. Their mind does not constantly seek to repeat the same activity and is at peace. Addiction and conditioning of the mind do not take hold of them. Such people enjoy every activity to the fullest; they remain happy and peaceful throughout their lives.

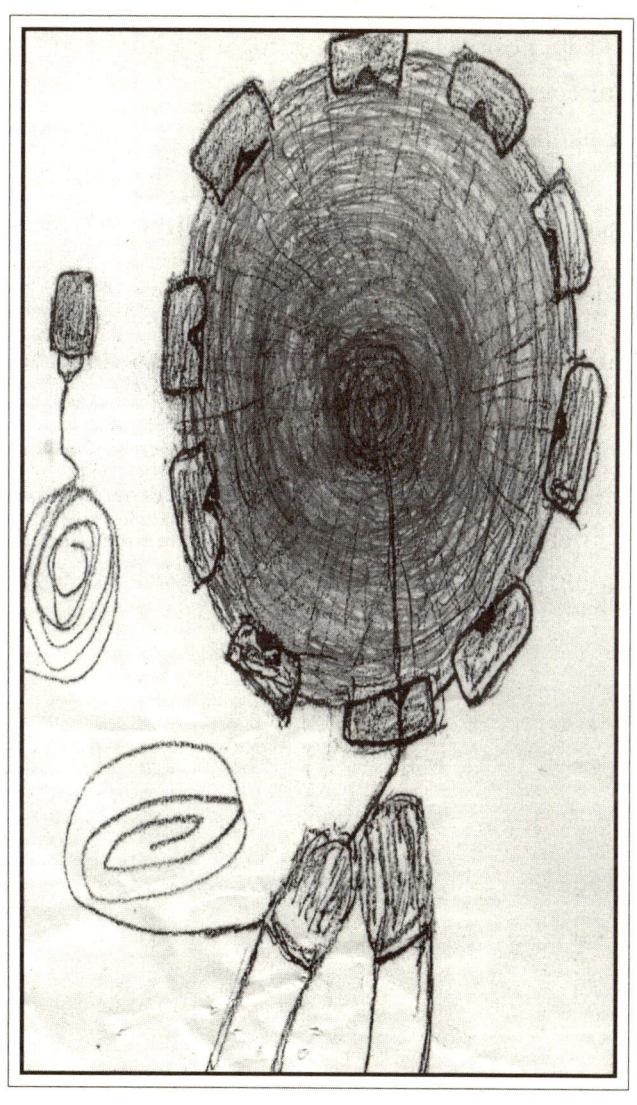

Just like the constant movement of a rope can create a groove in the stone, the constant racing of our mind can create a habit that we slip into easily. This conditioning can be a source of misery.

They radiate positive energy, creating a positive environment for themselves and those around them.

The nature of the mind can be compared to fetching water from a well. The deeper the water level in the well, the more movement there is of the rope on the surface of the stone, creating a deeper groove that makes it harder to take the rope out. However, when the water level rises to the edge of the well, there is no longer a need for the rope and stone, you can directly fill the bucket with water.

Similarly, the lower a person's energy level or self-awareness, the more conditioned their mind becomes. But when a person's energy level is full, their mind always remains deconditioned, allowing them to live freely.

3

FALSE PERCEPTION OF 'I' PUSHES HUMANS INTO A DREAMWORLD

Sage Vashishta told Rama that this world we perceive through our senses is not real, but a manifestation of the Creator's cosmic dream. However, with the emergence of the ego or 'I', it appears utterly real. Just like a dreamer is unaware of the fleeting nature of the objects seen in the dream, the same holds true for the cosmic dream of the Creator. We are oblivious to the transitory nature of the world around us.

The Sage asked Rama to consider the following scenario:

You are sitting in front of me with your eyes and ears open, looking at me and listening to me intently. What happens when your attention gets distracted, wandering off to some other thought or idea? You cannot see me or listen to me. Despite being physically present and with your sensory organs available, you are unable to perceive me without your active attention. What does it mean? If your eyes had the power to see properly and your ears had the power to listen, they should have performed their functions without requiring you to pay attention. That, however, does not happen. Without attention, the entire body becomes like a statue. What happens when your attention is activated? Once again, your eyes start seeing me and your ears start listening to me. What does it mean? It means that without attention, the eyes cannot see, the ears cannot listen, the mouth cannot speak, the tongue cannot taste, the nose cannot smell, the hands cannot move, and the feet cannot walk. This means that your body needs attention—the power of the self—to function.

Our body, mind and intellect are parts of a machine that runs on the energy of the self, which is infinite consciousness. This energy of the self is not exclusive to humans. All living beings, including plants, birds, animals and insects, possess it. Even non-living entities have it. This energy of the self is present in each and every particle of the universe. It is omnipresent.

When we consider that our body, mind and intellect operate as a machine that runs on the energy of the self, the question of whether 'I' truly exists arises. A machine cannot be an 'I', and this suggests that the concept of the self is an illusion. Instead, it is the infinite consciousness that exists. It is the energy of the self which sees through eyes, listens through ears, speaks through the mouth, tastes through the tongue, smells through the nose, works through hands and walks through feet, thinks through the intellect, gains knowledge through the brain, and so on. Not just that. It is the power of the self that keeps the whole universe alive.

The question that arises then is: Who we are?

It is now very clear that we are not a machine called a body; we are the energy of the self. Not only us, but everything in the universe is the energy of the self. This energy is present in all facets of the universe, whether living or non-living, and whether it has form or is formless. This reality underscores the oneness of the universe and reminds us that we are connected to all things.

'I' does not truly exist. When we identify ourselves exclusively with our body, our perception creates a false sense of ownership, birthing a false notion of 'mine' and furthering the development of a false ego. This may lead us to perceive a false world, disconnected from the true world of unconditional manifestation, and cause us to become trapped in the illusory dreamworld.

When a false ego convinces us that we are the doer and can do whatever we want, we are tossed into the material world. We start pursuing material objects and seeking physical pleasures for our gratification. However, this ever-receding goal creates a never-ending chase which leads us away from the energy of the self. As a result, the remaining energy of the self dwindles, making us energy deficient.

The depletion of the positive energy of the self traps us in a negative cycle of bondage and misery. This deficiency leads to a life of stress, restlessness, worry and fear. Although we want to escape this hell, we do not know how to break free from this vicious cycle of negativity.

4

GREAT MASTER NAGARJUNA

A young man, overwhelmed by a sense of restlessness, sought out Master Nagarjuna for relief. The wise master told him to first understand the nature of his restlessness, before seeking a solution. The master told him that the root of his restlessness was his own self-created bondage or clinging, which he perceived as a reality. This perception was a result of his own ignorance. The master assured him that once he acknowledged this truth, he could emerge from his state of restlessness with ease. However, the young man remained unconvinced. How, he wondered, could one create his own bondage and then expect someone else to relieve him of it? The master insisted that ignorance leads people to create their own misery, including bondage and restlessness. But again, the young man did not agree.

The master suggested a test to the young man to experience bondage and understand the root cause of restlessness. The young man wanted to know what test he had to undergo. The master instructed him to sit in solitude and recite a mantra with his eyes closed for three days continuously without food and water. If he was ready for such a test, he would learn the greatest secret behind why people experience restlessness and suffering, and how it is their own doing.

The young man felt anxious and agreed to take the test. He asked the master where he should sit for three days and what mantra had to be recited. The master showed him a cave in a mountain near his monastery. The young man was instructed to close his eyes and recite the words 'I am a buffalo' with full concentration for three whole days. He could not take a break or have food and water. The young man laughed at the ridiculousness of the mantra. The master told him to follow the instructions without making any objections.

The young man was determined and went to the cave to take the test. He sat there and began reciting the mantra as instructed by the master, completely engrossed in his practice. He started saying 'I am a buffalo' over and over. At first, he felt that it was all nonsense. But then he remembered the words of the master. Eager to know the greatest secret behind restlessness, he started reciting the mantra with renewed determination. He followed all the instructions.

After one day and one night, the young man started experiencing strange sensations. A buffalo appeared before his

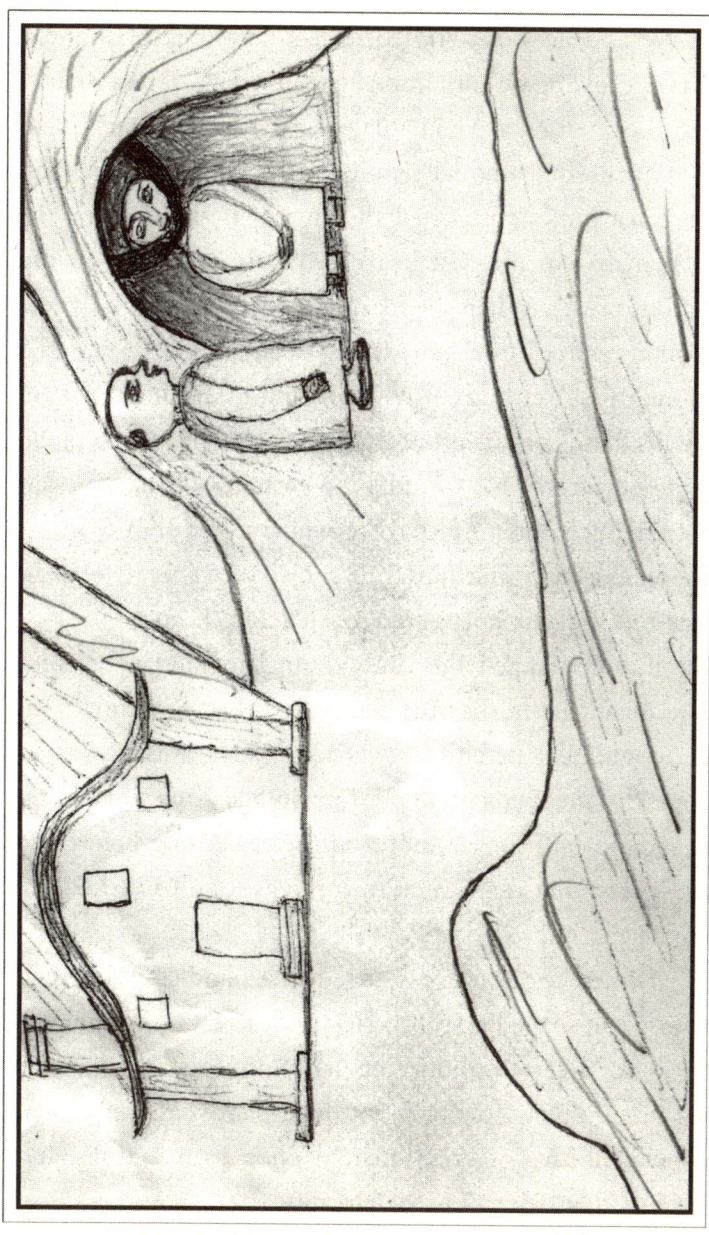

Master Nagarjuna asks a young man to continuously recite a mantra inside a cave to understand the root cause of restlessness.

mind's eye and his body started to feel heavier. Horns and a tail started growing out of him. After three days of persistently reciting the mantra, a vivid image of a fully grown buffalo with big horns appeared in his mind as if he was in a dream. Master Nagarjuna approached the cave and shouted for the young man to emerge. On hearing the first call, the young man did not react. When the master shouted more loudly, the young man realized that someone was calling out to him. The young man rose from his seated position as a buffalo would, placing his hands on the ground first before standing up on all fours. He began to walk towards the entrance of the cave but did not emerge. When Master Nagarjuna asked him to come out, the young man murmured in a low voice that he wanted to come out, but his horns were obstructing him.

The master slapped the young man hard and asked him what he meant by horns. The slap jolted the young man out of the dreamlike state and he realized that he was no longer experiencing the perception of the buffalo—there were no horns and no buffalo. He found himself standing before the master. The young man came to his senses and touched the feet of the master.

He claimed to have experienced first-hand how his own perception can shape his reality. He discovered that continuous perception of a certain thing can cause him to start feeling as though it were real, despite it not having any basis in reality. He concluded that it is ultimately one's own actions and perceptions that determine their reality.

The young man was thrilled to discover that his life was truly in his own hands. He realized that his perception shaped his reality, so he could choose to make his life good by focusing on positive things, or he could choose to make it miserable by focusing on negativity. He also recognized that his attachment, bondage and clinging were the root causes of his negative perceptions, which bred feelings of restlessness, fear and worry—all of which were illusory. Moreover, he discovered that his perception was powered by the energy of the self, and that he would become what he perceived. He finally understood why people were restless—it was their own doing. The young man was overjoyed to have discovered this great secret.

Master Nagarjuna pointed out to the young man that his belief of being a buffalo was only three days old, so it was relatively easy to awaken him by smacking his face. The young man emerged from his sleep easily and realized that he was not a buffalo but a human being. Master Nagarjuna then proceeded to explain that people have been perceiving their body as 'I' for many lifetimes, possibly spanning thousands of years. Their perception has hardened over time like steel, making it difficult to awaken them from their prolonged slumber. This is why people suffer and lead miserable lives, as they continue to cling to this false belief. The deep grooves of their perception have become so ingrained that even if they come to understand that their body is not actually their 'I', the rope of their perception continues to be stuck, and they remain trapped in their old ways of thinking and living.

The young man, now even more curious, asked Master Nagarjuna if there was a way to awaken people from their long slumber. The master explained to the young man that in order to awaken him further, he would have to undertake a practical exercise—meditation. Through meditation, the young man would be able to experience a state beyond perception, leading him to an understanding of the truth, infinite consciousness, superpower and the Creator. He would realize that the energy of the self is what gives birth, runs the entire life cycle, and takes back life to begin again. Meditation would enable him to reconnect with the source that he was once connected with at the time of his birth and in early childhood. Through knowing the self, he would come to know what he truly is. He would realize that he is not the 'I' or the body but rather the ultimate reality—the energy of the self that runs the entire universe. The master further explained that it was through perception that he was losing valuable moments of his life, but by meditating, he could overcome this and awaken from his slumber to the truth of who he really is.

Once someone reconnects with their self through meditation, they will realize their freedom, bliss and power. This will make them truly happy. Life will become effortless, and they will find enjoyment in everything. They will understand how perception only leads to misery, and slowly awaken from their long sleep as their self rises further and further. This will allow them to fully realize the false nature of the ego's perception of 'I', and how it creates the illusion of 'mine'. It is the combination of 'I' and 'mine' that gives rise to the false material world of perception, which engulfs one's life in bondage and misery.

Upon hearing about meditation, the young man asked the master to explain what it was. The master explained to him how meditation involves using the breath to silence the mind, and how this can facilitate reconnection with the energy of the self. The young man followed the master's instructions and began to meditate, eventually becoming reconnected with his self (enlightened). The master then told him that if he were to continue meditating regularly, he would eventually be able to hear the sound of silence continuously—which is the sound of the self. Through this continued practice, his energy of the self would also be enhanced, and he would begin to lead a stress-free life of freedom and bliss.

5

THE BALANCING ACT

If one suddenly realizes that despite acquiring material wealth and benefits, they still lack absolute peace and joy, they may feel lost and wonder what went wrong and where. The answer is that they may have missed the balancing act.

The imbalance between material and cosmic energy (our spirit) can create a void that cannot be filled with material wealth or sensual pleasures. This void can only be filled with the cosmic energy of the self.

The tragedy of human existence is that we tend to comprehend the world solely through our senses. We believe that we perceive the world solely through our senses but fail to consider the power that runs through them. We indulge in physical pleasures and experiences but never know the true experiencer behind them. Our minds wander and entertain thoughts, yet we do not know the true thinker behind our intellect. We focus on accumulating knowledge through our brains but neglect the real knower behind it. In essence, we confine ourselves to understanding the physical world through our bodies and minds, but we fail to recognize the operator of these bodies and minds.

The knowledge and beliefs that people possess are merely a small part of their selves, which is physical. However, they remain unaware of the greater part that is beyond the physical and worth knowing. The question arises, how can someone who knows so little about their self be truly happy?

To find happiness, one needs to understand themselves and come out of the state of misery. Only when they come to know about themselves can they realize that they have been leading a life of ignorance. They may have wasted the power of their self for nothing and are currently living a life with minimal energy.

Once they understand the reality, they may realize that they have been exhausting their precious energy on irrelevant things while obsessing about the outside world. Their minds have been conditioned to focus on materialistic things and physical pleasures, leading to a heavy drain of the cosmic energy of the self through their bodily senses.

To fill the void in their lives, individuals need to restore balance and reverse the cycle. Instead of expending energy, they need to conserve it. Instead of thinking about external things, they need to remain still. The energy of the self is always at rest and by remaining at rest, this energy will begin to fill the void naturally. The energy of the self is abundant and present everywhere.

To restore lost energy and achieve a vast amount of energy, individuals need to recollect themselves and reconnect with their inner source through meditation. By gradually restoring balance and replenishing energy, they can enter the true world of endless bliss, peace and happiness.

To ensure that the conservation and restoration of energy become a regular practice, it is necessary to keep in mind the following points:

1. Let go of the false perception of the ego and strive to be ego-less. This will help you conserve the energy of the self that would otherwise go to waste.
2. The world we see around us manifests automatically, running without our efforts. By removing ego and being effortless, we can save energy that would otherwise have been expended.
3. Thoughts are powered by the energy of the self, and positive thoughts lead to positive outcomes while negative thoughts waste energy. Focusing on positive thoughts conserves energy and brings happiness.
4. The energy of the self is the universe itself, and there is no 'other'. Doing good for others is the same as doing good for oneself, conserving energy and promoting happiness.

5. Going against our consciousness leads to the universe going against us, while supporting it leads to the universe supporting us.

6. When we observe our thoughts, the negative ones disappear. This saves us energy.

7. Restlessness, worries, fears and stress are not real but imaginary. Conserving the energy of the self can make them disappear.

8. Speaking, seeing, hearing and thinking consume a large part of the energy of the self. By being mindful of that, we can conserve our energy.

9. Doubts give rise to negative thinking and waste precious energy.

10. The physical body and the self work harmoniously and joyfully as a perfect natural combination. The false perception of the ego, however, interrupts this compatibility, leading to suffering and a drain on energy.

11. Health issues, both physical and mental, often arise from a low level of energy of the self. The root cause of all sickness is the ego or the false perception of 'I' that drains the energy of the self and causes restlessness, leading to illness. With a high level of energy, a person's breathing becomes deeper, smoother and longer, resulting in healthy organs.

12. As a child, you were fully connected to the cosmic source of energy of the self, and a stream of consciousness

flowed within you, keeping you energetic, peaceful, happy and joyful. However, with growth, your mind developed and you were distracted by it. You forgot the stream of consciousness and became disconnected from the cosmic source. You became dependent on the energy within you, which further got drained by running your mind in all directions, leading to restlessness, worries and fears. This happened due to ignorance.

After attaining knowledge, the cycle can be reversed. Through meditation, you can reconnect with your cosmic source, and the stream of consciousness will start flowing within you, raising your self-control and allowing you to contain any distractions. Your mind will start coming back to rest, and a further rise in the level of self will take you into the continuous flow of energy of the self as it was in childhood. You will regain your energy of the self, leading you to absolute peace and joy. The main purpose is to live in harmony and oneness with the whole universe which is your true nature. By doing so, you can have an abundance of the energy of the self, allowing you to lead a true life of freedom and eternal bliss.

6

ANNIHILATION OF 'I' WILL MAKE PLANET EARTH THE 'HOUSE OF GODS'

It is ironic that human beings suffer from a deficiency of the energy that is abundantly available everywhere in the universe. This is akin to a fish in the ocean suffering from a scarcity of water. The energy of the self is present everywhere and yet people are living their lives in restlessness due to their ignorance about their true nature.

Despite the advancements in science and technology, people are still suffering because they lack knowledge about the energy of the self. However, wherever people who are full of this energy have lived or meditated, those places have remained peaceful and full of vibrations of positive energy even after many years. People visit such places as a pilgrimage to raise their energy levels and find peace.

Secluded places like mountains, where there is no pollution from human activity, vibrate with positive energy in contrast to places where there is a lot of traffic. If you visit such a place, you will feel calm and peaceful.

It is, however, not necessary to go to any such place to find peace. Instead, one needs to learn how to connect with oneself and raise one's energy level to achieve peace wherever one is.

While the twentieth century has seen an explosion of scientific discoveries and technological advancements that have made human life easier, the rapid increase in human population has put a strain on the environment, leading to pollution, global warming and a deterioration in the level of energy of the self. If not taken care of, the more advancements we make, the more our quality of life will deteriorate.

Our focus has been on the outer aspects of the quality of life, such as the reduction of labour, quicker movement, easy communication, luxurious living and longevity. We neglect the inner facets of the quality of life, such as the reduction of fear, anxiety, restlessness, worries and stress levels. What is the point of achieving a long life under pressure, restlessness and worries?

Scientific discoveries and advancements in technology alone cannot make people happier, and the inner quality of life must be discovered. The population explosion is both a cause and a result of the deterioration of the inner quality of life. The root of all problems on the planet is the deficiency of energy of the self or the infinite consciousness in human beings. Millions of people are living with negative energy resulting from this deficiency, leading to fear, stress, restlessness and worries. Although people assume their worries, stress and restlessness are due to external factors, they are, in reality, due to a lack of positive energy.

It is crucial to understand that all scientific discoveries and technological developments originate from the energy of the self. Medical advancements, technological developments, and all the developments we see around us have been birthed by the energy of the self. As a society, we have learned to conserve our energy for development, but, regrettably, we have also learned to fritter away that energy in acquisition and physical pleasures. Human beings have discarded this valuable energy to such an extent that it has led to a severe deficit of this energy on Earth. This energy deficit is causing problems like pollution, global warming, crime, conflicts, terrorism and oppression.

It is possible for people to reverse the cycle of throwing away the energy of the self. Instead, they can learn to bring in or conserve it. Raising this energy to the level of annihilating the 'I' will make scientific discoveries and technological advancements effortless. All the problems that exist on Earth will come to an end, and our planet will become a centre of pilgrimage known as 'The House of Gods'.

7

SELF OR SOUL

In the *Vedas* and *Upanishads*, the self is described in the following manner:

I am the Absolute Being (Brahman): *sat*

In a state of consciousness: *chit*

In eternal bliss: *ananda*

The self is called 'sat chit ananda' (or 'sachidanand' in short). The Absolute Being, Brahman, is the omnipresent truth and conscious observer of everything that exists. Brahman is always present, from the beginning and will forever remain so. It exists in a state of constant rest, everlasting happiness and joy.

Our true self is not confined to the body, but rather, the body is within the self. The entire universe that we see with our eyes is not outside of us, but rather within the self. Space and time are also positioned within the self, and as such, the self (soul) or infinite consciousness contains everything, and nothing exists outside of it.

The true nature of the self is freedom, and it is constant, alone, unchanging, at rest, uniform, indestructible, eternal, untouchable, invisible, self-illuminating, permanent and pure.

Indeed, the self is omnipresent, omniscient and omnipotent. It is the only thing that exists, and it is through the self that everything is accomplished using our bodies. When we allow the self to work without interference from our 'I', we are in a state of perfect living and being. Our energy of the self flows effortlessly, and we are full of its powers.

However, when our 'I' interferes with the self, we allow our bodies to influence it. As a result, our energy of the self goes to waste through the material world's pull of gravity, which is our perception. We enter a world of materialism and lose our superpower, starting to live a life of illusions and dreams. The real challenge humanity faces is to transcend these illusions and lead a life of eternal bliss and freedom.

A life of no effort is possible, where we witness everything and allow things to happen spontaneously, being at complete rest from within. In such a life, we experience lasting peace and happiness, and we are free to enjoy living. We must learn to conserve and bring in the priceless energy of the self, mitigate negative energies, and manage our energy levels to achieve this state of being. Only then will we experience everlasting joy and transcendence.

8

SAGE VASHISHTA

Yoga Vashishta has written about Sage Vashishta. The musings are deeply relevant.

Here are some glimpses of what he has written:

Sage Vashishta: O Rama, remain unattached and endowed with the spirit of renunciation and with the realization that whatever you do or experience is an offering to the omnipresent being, Brahman. Then you will realize the truth, and that will be the end of all doubts. What appears to be the world here is the magic (the work) of the infinite consciousness. There is no unity here, nor is there duality. My instructions, too, are of the same nature. The words, their meanings, the disciple who receives them, their wish or the effort they put in, and the guru's ability to use these words are all part of the play of the energy of the infinite consciousness. In the peace of one's own inner being, consciousness vibrates and world vision arises. The absence of this vibration means that there will be no world vision. The mind is merely a movement in consciousness. Failure to realize this truth leads to world vision and exacerbates the movement of thought in consciousness. Ignorance and mental activity feed off each other. However, when inner intelligence is awakened, the craving for pleasure ceases. One recognizes that it is the energy of the self that experiences the experiences.

The desire for liberation can interfere with the fullness of self, whereas the lack of such desire may promote bondage. Therefore, it is preferable to cultivate constant awareness. The movement in consciousness is the sole cause for both bondage and liberation. Becoming aware of this movement can help to end it. When one becomes aware of the ego, it ceases, for it has no support anymore. At this point, one may ask, who is bound by whom, or who is liberated by whom?

༄

Prince Rama to Sage Vashishta: O Sage, just like the cities we see during our dreams are unreal, isn't the world—the dream of Brahma, the Creator—equally unreal and illusory?

Sage Vashishta: The belief in the reality of this creation destroys true perception. However, due to the emergence of the ego-sense, it appears solidly real. Just as a dreamer does not realize the evanescence of the objects seen in a dream, so

Sage Vashishta tells Rama that the words, their meanings, the disciple who receives them, their wish or the effort they put in, and the guru's ability to use these words are all part of the play of the energy of the infinite consciousness.

it is with the cosmic dream of the Creator. The dream reflects the characteristics of the dreamer. And that which is born of the unreal must also be unreal. Although this world appears real, it is born of an unreal concept: the dream of the Creator. Therefore, it must be firmly rejected.

The creation appears momentarily in the infinite consciousness, that is the self. During that moment, the illusory notion of its long duration arises, causing it to seem real. However, nothing is truly real, nor is anything truly unreal. All is made possible everywhere in this dream known as creation. Just as one immersed in a dream sees that dream as utterly real, so too one immersed in this creation sees it as utterly real. And just as one goes from one dream to another, one goes from one delusion to another delusion, thus experiencing the world as utterly real.

∽

A BEAUTIFUL INCIDENT IN THE LIFE OF SAGE VASHISHTA

Rishi Vishwamitra was furious with Sage Vashishta for not granting him the status of 'Brahman Rishi', the ultimate spiritual attainment. Vishwamitra believed he deserved the title but was convinced that Sage Vashishta was withholding it out of jealousy. The matter became the talk of the town, and Vishwamitra grew increasingly impatient. Eventually, he resorted to extreme measures, taking his sword and setting off to the ashram of Sage

Vashishta with the intention of killing him.

As Sage Vashishta addressed his disciples in the courtyard, Rishi Vishwamitra lay in wait, concealed behind a bush, waiting for the opportune moment when the Sage would be alone. After the address, there was a question hour when the disciples were invited to ask questions to clarify their doubts.

One of the disciples asked Sage Vashishta why he had not pronounced Rishi Vishwamitra a Brahman Rishi when he deserved the title. Sage Vashishta patiently replied that although he had been waiting to bestow the title for some time, there was still one flaw left to address.

The disciple enquired as to what flaw remained. Sage Vashishta explained to the disciple the weakness that needed to be addressed. As a member of the warrior clan, Rishi Vishwamitra had a tendency to resort to violence over small matters, and he had not yet fully surrendered himself. If he were pronounced a Brahman Rishi without rectifying this flaw, it would hold him back from making progress.

The disciple was content with this explanation. Meanwhile, Rishi Vishwamitra, who had been eavesdropping behind the bush, heard every word and was overcome by the Sage's kindness. All of his anger dissipated as he realized his mistake. He threw away his sword and rushed to Sage Vashishta, touching his feet in humility.

The sage stopped him, embraced him, and pronounced him a Brahman Rishi. But Rishi Vishwamitra felt unworthy of the title and apologized, revealing that he had come with the intent

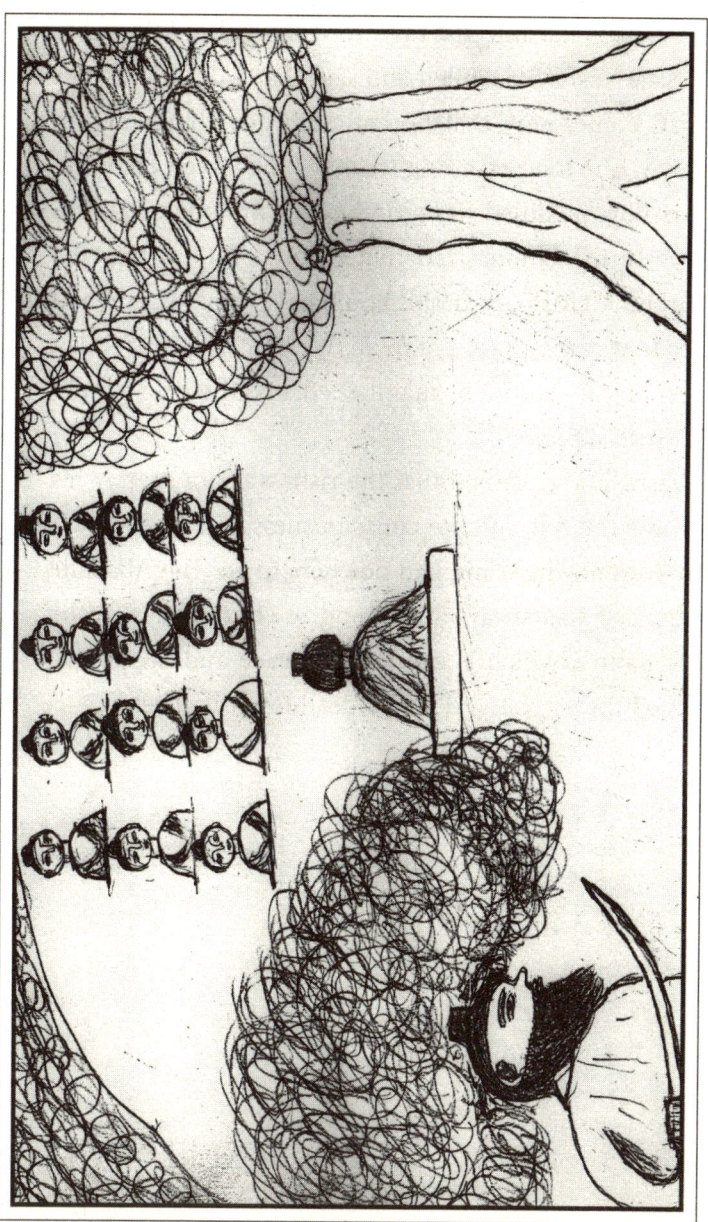

Rishi Vishwamitra was furious with Sage Vashishta for not granting him the status of 'Brahman Rishi'. He took his sword and set off to the ashram of the sage with the intention of killing him.

to kill Sage Vashishta, and that his sword was behind the bush. However, Sage Vashishta smiled and said that it did not matter how he had come, only that he had surrendered his ego to the Brahman. The long-standing weakness had been resolved, and he was now qualified to be declared a Brahman Rishi.

Sage Vashishta emphasized that before pronouncing the status of Brahman Rishi, the rishi should have fully surrendered their ego to the omnipresent Brahman. Without such surrender, the 'fullness of self' cannot be maintained, and the rishi cannot realize his true nature.

Sage Vashishta explained that the rishi was not merely his body—he was the self, infinite consciousness and Creator. He had come from nowhere and had nowhere to go. The Absolute Being of the self was always at rest and in eternal bliss. To be in his true nature, which is everlasting peace and happiness, the rishi must be at rest and surrender his ego entirely.

9

THE WITNESS

The omnipresent being Brahman, infinite consciousness or self is an observer or witness. Our true nature is to witness, and we can stay in the fullness of self if we become witnesses. However, when we identify with the ego and become 'I', everything goes wrong. The ego takes charge of our witnessing power, stripping it of doer-ship and ownership. It directs us towards a craving for pleasures, causing us to forget our true nature of witnessing. In reality, the pleasures we seek are just a drop of water in the ocean of the self.

To regain the fullness of the self, we can reverse the order and drop the ego to become witnesses again. Through witnessing our thoughts, actions and pleasures, we realize that we are not the doers or owners of anything. The pleasures we are seeking are simply a waste of the energy of the self. As we regain our lost energy, our witnessing power becomes stronger, and we start coming out of misery to enjoy life again. When we reach the fullness of the energy of the self, we enter everlasting peace and happiness, which is our true immortal nature.

At this stage, while doing everything, we are doing nothing because we are not putting in any effort. We have become a pure witness, which is our true nature of unconditional manifestation.

10

THE NEED FOR AN AWAKENING

Our life is wholly dependent on the energy of the self and nothing else. This energy of the self is our attention or *dhyaan*. Our mind and body come into existence because of the energy of the self. All the powers that seem to exist within our personality originate from energy of the self. The amount of power we have depends on the energy of the self. The lesser the energy of the self, the lesser are our powers.

We are all born to live fearless, independent, healthy, wealthy, wise, free, contented, compassionate, impartial and lovable lives. However, a decrease in the level of the energy of the self pushes us into the realm of fear, dependency, sickness, poverty, foolishness, dishonour, suspicion, restlessness, dishonesty, slavery, discontentment, narrow-mindedness, duality and hatred.

This all happens because of the pull of material gravity working on our energy of the self. Our feelings, thoughts and emotions are subtle materials. Their movement in our energy of the self constitutes our minds. These movements occupy our energy of the self. The more movements there are, the more energy is used up, and the less energy is left for daily living. As our energy of the self decreases, it creates a deficiency of positive energy in the system. All our fears, restlessness and worries are created because of this deficiency of positive energy (energy of the self).

The day we are able to grasp this fact is the day we can start conserving our energy, which we have been unnecessarily wasting. Further, we can put in efforts to regain our lost energy so that it becomes abundant once again, enabling us to live peacefully and experience ananda.

We were born to live in abundance of energy of the self, and to achieve this, we must remain always connected to the self (source). When we are connected to the self, material gravity cannot decrease the level of energy in our system, and we remain full of energy of the self. This is our true nature: 'sat chit ananda'.

11

UNCONDITIONAL MANIFESTATION

Everything in this universe is happening on its own. It is all effortless. The sun and the moon rise and set. Plants grow and bear flowers and fruits. Birds eat, chirp, mate, and feed their chicks. Animals graze, hunt, mate, and care for their young ones. Rivers flow thousands of kilometres to meet the ocean. Stars shine and seasons change. The entire universe is running without effort and any intervention from humans.

In human experience, the need for effort arises due to the false perception of the 'I' or ego, which drains the energy of the self. This false perception makes us feel powerless, requiring us to put in effort to do everything. However, the moment we drop the ego, we become powerful and effortless. We become one with the universe and follow its natural rhythm.

This whole universe is full of energy of the self. It is always at rest. When we do things effortlessly, we come to rest from within, and the energy of the self starts rushing in to fill the void. This is similar to how air at high pressure flows towards low pressure to fill the void. As the energy of the self fills us up, we achieve fullness of the self.

Human life is the greatest contradiction ever. When we identify ourselves as 'I', we do not truly exist. However, when we realize ourselves as the self or soul, we see that we exist in everything. At once, we are nothing and everything. The journey of life is to traverse this distance from nothing to everything.

Our problem is that we seek permanence in impermanence. The world, however, is always changing. Since change is permanent, we need to change with the change. The material world keeps changing because of the constraints of space and time. Seeking permanence here is an exercise in futility. When the energy of the self is high, we go beyond space and time. Then, change does not affect us.

The mind, ego and the world we perceive with our senses are all products of space and time. However, when we transcend these limitations, we enter the world of permanence, which is a state of blissful consciousness known as ananda. The root of all suffering in human life is the ego, which is a figment of our imagination. The ego creates an illusory world that leads to suffering, fear, restlessness, worry and stress. We can escape this imagined world by increasing our level of self-energy, which removes the ego from our consciousness. When we let go of the ego, we enter a state of fullness that is real and abiding. This state of being is characterized by everlasting peace, happiness and joy. This world of ananda is the true reality, beyond life and death, where there is no suffering or transience.

12

RAMAKRISHNA'S TEACHINGS FOR THE ENLIGHTENED ONES

THE OBSERVER IS THE OBSERVED

Enlightenment reveals that we are cosmic energy, never born, and omnipresent. This energy—Brahman—is self-knowing and the force behind creation, operation and destruction. Impossible to touch, move or affect, this energy powers the entire universe. The visible universe is simply an illusion of this energy of the self.

Just as a seed grows into a tree, powered by the cosmic energy of the self, the universe blooms and thrives. With time, the tree blossoms, bearing fruit, all thanks to the power of the self. At every moment, its existence is due to the energy of the self, rendering it inseparable from the cosmic energy.

An enlightened individual realizes that 'the observer is the observed', a concept reminiscent of the Buddhist saying 'man sees the mountain and mountain sees the man'.

In essence, a tree loaded with fruits is nothing but the energy of the self.

When a seed is sown in fertile soil, it grows into a tree, powered by the cosmic energy of the self. With proper time, a seedling emerges, followed by leaves, stems, branches, and eventually fruits. Every moment of the tree's existence is sustained by the energy of the self. In essence, the tree and its fruits are nothing but the energy of the self.

An enlightened individual observing this tree sees beyond what meets the eye—they see the energy of the self sustaining it, and the beauty of that energy. Simultaneously, they observe themselves observing the tree, recognizing that both are manifestations of the energy of the self. This leads them to conclude that 'the observer is the observed', a concept reminiscent of the Buddhist saying 'man sees the mountain and mountain sees the man'.

The energy of the self observes everything in the universe, from the tiniest particles to the vast expanse of the cosmos. This concept of observation is captured in the Buddhist Heart Sutra, which states, 'emptiness is form and form is emptiness'.

Enlightenment involves understanding what is real and what is not, and connecting with the truth of the cosmic energy of the self. As a person becomes more attuned to this reality, their attachment to the illusory aspects of the world begins to weaken. They start to enjoy the presence of the real, and become more like an observer of the unreal that they continue to observe.

CHOICELESS AWARENESS

Awareness is a special gift bestowed upon humans by Mother Nature, which is commonly referred to as free will. Unlike any other species, humans can choose their path in life. Their choices determine their life because they have the power of free will. However, due to ignorance and the influence of the materialistic world, humans often choose a life solely based on the material senses rather than embracing their true nature, which is beyond the five senses.

They chase temporary pleasures and forget their true nature of freedom, eternal bliss, everlasting peace, happiness and joy. Their wrong choices lead them to a life of sorrow, bondage and misery. They face a dilemma where they want to continue making choices, but they also desire to get rid of the sorrows they are experiencing. Unfortunately, it is impossible to live a life of everlasting peace and continue to make the same choices that led them to a life of misery.

To attain everlasting peace, humans must surrender their choices by letting go of the perceived power of their ego. The choices they make are fuelled by the non-existent 'I', which takes them far away from their true nature. Their choices plunge them into a life of perception, distancing them from the real life. They end up living a false life and cycling through births and deaths without finding true happiness.

In one's true nature, there is no birth, karma or ego. To live a life in everlasting peace and joy, the only solution is 'choiceless awareness'. This concept is known as 'Do Not Judge' in Buddhism because, by judging, one is making a choice.

People living in the material world may wonder how they can live a life without choices or judgements. The solution for them is to drop their 'I' or ego and enter their true nature. Their true nature operates automatically according to the will of the energy of the self. It is no longer their choice, but instead, it is the choice of the energy of the self. Likewise, it is no longer their judgement, but instead, it is the judgement of the energy of the self. The energy of the self operates spontaneously.

It is the choices or judgments made through the 'I' or ego that bring about restlessness, worries and fears. Once a person drops their 'I' or ego, they become choiceless while making choices. They also become non-judgemental while judging everything, allowing them to live a life free from the burdens of the ego.

'I', ego and mind are the same thing. They keep a person occupied with the pursuit of material possessions and physical pleasures, which are merely drops of water in the vast ocean of one's true nature. This persistent pursuit drains the energy of the self, leading to a restless state.

When a person acknowledges that the energy of the self provides everlasting peace and joy, they can find internal rest and move beyond the 'I'. They learn to remain present and accepting of their current situation and themselves. They let go of their attachments, content with living in the fullness of the self and becoming ego-less. This opens the door to the world of 'Choiceless Awareness', where they can enjoy a fulfilled life of eternal peace, happiness and joy.

PART-2

EXPERIENCE LIFE BEYOND SPACE AND TIME

The human experience of absolute peace and happiness lies beyond the limitations of space and time. Just as darkness is a mere illusion in the absence of light, the world we see as solid and real is nothing but an illusion in the absence of the energy of the self or infinite consciousness.

Human beings are born into a world that exists beyond the constraints of space and time. However, due to the identification of the body as 'I', we fall into the illusory world of space and time. This world is ever-changing, impermanent and transitory. Hence, it is the source of suffering.

When people connect with the source of infinite consciousness and start living in the abundance of the energy of the self, they move beyond the limitations of space and time. The same world that was once a source of suffering and impermanence becomes a world of bliss for them. They are no longer affected by the changing nature of the world, but instead find themselves in a state of eternal bliss. If every person on this planet were to have an abundance of the energy of the self, it would become a heavenly abode.

13

ENERGY OF THE SELF AND MATTER ENERGY

The Hindu philosopher Shri Adi Shankaracharya described how the five elements emerged from the energy of the self or infinite consciousness. He says that space emerged from the self or soul, air emerged from space, fire emerged from air, water emerged from fire, and the earth emerged from water.

These five elements make up the whole universe or material world, which can be seen with our eyes. The diversity of our universe arises from the permutations and combinations of these elements in various proportions.

Buddhism teaches us that if we were to enlarge the image of any object, such as an apple, under a microscope, we would eventually reach a point where the distinction between the apple and its environment would disappear. This highlights the essential unity of all things in the universe, which are ultimately made up of the same basic elements. Although things may appear different and separate at first glance, these differences are ultimately superficial and do not reflect the fundamental reality of the universe.

According to science, the interaction between electromagnetism and gravity can transform energy into matter, which is ultimately confined by the constraints of space and time. From the descriptions provided, we can surmise that electromagnetism and gravity are responsible for creating the diversity in the universe through the combination of the same underlying elements that emerge from the energy of the self.

Matter energy is the dead end of the energy of the self. It has all the properties opposite to the energy of the self.

Energy of Self	Matter Energy
Invisible witnessing self	Visible and non-visible (seen or witnessed)
Constant	Variable
Alone	Diversified
Uniform	Non-uniform
Unchanging	Ever-changing
Untouchable	Touchable
Indestructible	Destructible
Self-illuminating	Dark matter

Permanent	Temporary
Pure	Impure
Eternal	Birth and death
Always at rest	Always restless
Non-dual	Full of dualities

A comparison of the energy of the self and matter energy reveals that as the energy of the self decreases in human beings, they tend to move towards matter energy. With the depletion of the energy of the self, human beings become vulnerable to the negative influence of their ego. This makes their behaviour as rigid as a stone.

14

GOLDEN CAGE OF GRAVITY

The most significant error that humanity has made is to identify their body as the 'I' or the self. This assumption has given rise to an entire world of material assumptions, as well as a virtual mental realm that is equally insubstantial. However, none of these—neither the 'I', the virtual mind, nor the material world—is real because they all fall under the influence of gravity. Consequently, our perception of life is shaped by the pull of gravity, which obfuscates our access to the truth and clouds our energy of the self. As a result, we become disconnected from the source of the self and live our lives with little access to abundant energy.

When we assume our body as the 'I', a multitude of assumptions arises. These assumptions span from our name and gender to our family, society, country, profession and skin colour. This list of assumptions drives us towards action, causing us to become a fervent 'doer'. Everything that we do gets stored in our memory, becoming past impressions or 'karmas'. These past impressions are composed of material experiences from past and present lives. Thus, the memory keeps growing and expanding, containing both positive impressions (being positive energy) and negative impressions (being negative energy). Positive impressions push us away from the pull of gravity, while negative impressions pull us down into gravity. This leads to a constant inner battle. This conflict gives rise to suffering, and often prompts humans to look for a way out. Our subconscious mind, which is essentially a collection of all these past impressions, governs everything in our life—from our behaviour and habits to our likes and dislikes and our overall perception of life. Ultimately, these assumptions keep us trapped in a cage of gravity.

Despite our efforts, we cannot escape this cage of gravity until we awaken to the reality that we have unknowingly trapped ourselves in it. Our minds often desire material objects, recognition, and physical pleasure, becoming addicted to them. With every addiction, our energy of the self declines even further, making it increasingly difficult to break free. Under the influence of gravity, our minds try to improve our physical living standards by pursuing luxurious material pleasures. We attempt to transform our cage of gravity into a golden cage of gravity, hoping to find happiness within it. However, this is a futile endeavour, as deep inside, we are aware that this pursuit is meaningless. We yearn to break free from this cage and regain our freedom.

There is a beautiful story:

Once a wealthy merchant found a young and beautiful parrot while he was travelling back home through a jungle. The merchant fell in love with the parrot and decided to keep it in a golden cage, decorated with precious items and comfortable cushions. He fed it with its favourite fruits and talked to it gently and lovingly. The parrot sang for its master, and the merchant became more and more attached to it over time.

One day, the merchant told the parrot that he was going on a tour that would pass through the same jungle where he had found it. He asked the parrot if it wanted to send a message to its loved ones. The parrot asked the merchant to convey this message: 'I am living in a golden cage of a wealthy merchant and I remember you.'

The merchant was delighted, thinking that the parrot was proud of its luxurious cage and his high reputation. He promised to deliver the message. However, upon reaching the jungle, the merchant saw a parrot fall from a tree as soon as he delivered the message. The merchant assumed that he had just informed the young parrot's mother. The mother parrot was shocked to hear the news and died instantly, leaving the merchant feeling sad and helpless.

When the merchant returned home, he told his beloved parrot what had happened. Suddenly, the parrot fell dead as well. The merchant was heartbroken to see his beloved parrot dead and threw its body out of the cage. However, he was amazed to see the parrot fly off and perch on a nearby tree. When the merchant asked the parrot what had happened, the parrot revealed that its mother had told it to pretend to be dead in order to escape the cage and attain freedom. Now, the parrot was a free bird, soaring through the sky where it belonged.

We don't need to pretend to be dead to escape the golden cage of gravity. We need to awaken to the reality that we are not the 'I', the ego, or even a physical body. We are the energy of the self, and we are constantly wasting our energy by striving for material objects and living in bondage and misery.

When we connect to our true self, we come to know that there is no mind, no material world, and no ego. It is the energy of the self that sees, hears, speaks, thinks, works and walks through us. We realize that we were never trapped in a cage of gravity, but always free to soar in the sky. With this awakening, we enter the real world of everlasting peace and happiness, where we belong.

15

THE SELF'S POWER OF CONCENTRATION

The self has the power of concentration, which we can use to gain clarity and understanding. When we focus our energy on a subject, our level of clarity rises as our energy increases. This principle can be applied to research and education, as well as in our personal lives.

We encourage our children to choose subjects they are passionate about and focus their energy on them. As they concentrate, they gain a greater understanding and can apply their knowledge to their careers. With time, as their level of energy increases, their ego decreases. The energy of the self is a positive force, while ego is negative. When positive energy rises, the negative ego becomes weaker, like darkness against light.

However, if someone focuses their energy with the goal of fulfilling their own greed, their ego will increase instead of decreasing. This can be harmful to the person and society, leading to greed, selfishness and narrow-mindedness.

When someone with a high level of energy of the self speaks to a large audience, people listen to the speaker with rapt attention. This is due to the speaker's clarity and understanding. However, if the speaker has low energy, they may not be heard.

The root cause of all human problems is a lack of awareness. We continue to suffer throughout our lives because we are not fully aware. This leads to a cycle of suffering life after life until we become fully aware.

Examples of awareness levels:

1) A man sitting in a room: He cannot see beyond the four walls of the room. He is a narrow-minded, greedy and selfish man with a very low awareness level. He suffers due to his inability to see beyond himself.

2) A man standing atop a clock tower with a high-powered telescope: He can see the entire city. He seems to be a free man experiencing an abundance of the energy of the Self. He is very clear about the world and situations. He enjoys life to the fullest.

3) Mother and child: A little child is busy playing with toys while his mother works in the kitchen. Even with the noise of his tiny footsteps, she can visualize which direction he's moving in and anticipate his intentions.

Although the child is connected to his source and has a higher awareness level than his mother, he still needs her supervision because his mind is not yet fully developed. He lacks reasoning and doesn't yet know right from wrong. To lead a joyful life in the material world, one requires not just a high awareness level but also a well-developed mind. A person needs both to live a happy life.

4) Various layers of the management system: In each and every field, different management systems are in operation. For example, in a manufacturing unit, there are workers, supervisors, managers, general manager, vice-president and president. All these levels are based on awareness levels.

5) A dimly lit room: A sudden bright light can make things that were previously unclear become visible. Similarly, when a person's awareness is low, they are unable to visualize things and situations with clarity and are prone to making wrong decisions. However, with a high awareness level, a person gains clarity about things and situations leading to making right decisions. Negative energy is not a thing but an illusion created in the absence of positive energy (energy of the self). In the same way, untruth is an illusion created in the absence of truth. To uncover the truth, we must eliminate the illusion by raising our energy of the self. By doing so, we can succeed in all areas of our lives.

16

TWO TYPES OF HUMAN MIND

Friedrich Schelling, the German philosopher, wrote: 'The mind sleeps in the stone, dreams in plant, awakens in the animal and becomes conscious in man, so mind is inherent in each particle of the universe.' Everything, from individuals to particles, receives an illumination of consciousness through the mind. The receptivity of the mind, in turn, determines the degree of consciousness. When the human mind is purified, it becomes highly receptive to consciousness, leading to its enlightenment.

Human mind is of two types:

1. Individual mind (virtual)
2. Universal Mind (real)

Every living being or non-living thing, except humans,

possesses only one type of mind, the Universal Mind. They all live in oneness with the universe. This allows them to live in unconditional manifestation and to experience harmony with the universe.

However, humans cannot live in oneness and therefore cannot live in harmony with the universe. This is the root cause of all problems. It is because their minds are divided into two parts: the real Universal Mind and the virtual individual mind.

1) The individual or virtual mind: It is developed out of ignorance when one assumes their body as the true 'I'. As the 'I' is just an assumption, it creates a false world of assumptions that separates one from the real world of unconditional manifestation. This false world includes notions of 'I', mine and ego, which together form a material world of imagination, far from reality. The virtual mind separates individuals from the universe by making them individualistic, leading them to a world of their own fantasies and perceptions. When seeing others, they perceive them as separate from themselves, leading them to believe they are the owner of themselves and can live a better life than others.

2) Universal mind: The individual mind of a person is a virtual mind that is contaminated with the impurities of 'I', mine and ego. These impurities develop into a virus of doer-ship. However, when the individual mind is purified, we become enlightened and come out of doer-

ship. The individual mind then vanishes, and we start to operate through the universal mind, which belongs to the whole universe. With the universal mind, we come back into the fold of oneness with the universe and start operating in harmony with it, leading us to live a life of ananda. The universal mind is the collective mind of the whole universe and operates in spontaneity or the present. When we are enlightened, we come out of our virtual mind and start living in the present. In the present, we exist in the soul that contains the past, the present and the future, and which is beyond the subconscious mind or the pull of gravity. In this stage, we return to our real destiny for which we were manifested.

∽

FANTASY OF THE VIRTUAL MIND

As the virtual mind of an individual receives consciousness from the source, which is the infinite consciousness, it starts to assume itself as the creator and enters into doer-ship, consequently developing an ego. As a result, every human lives within their tiny fantasy world, separate from the real world of oneness. When hundreds of crores of fantasy worlds exist parallel to the real world of oneness, they cloud the illumination of the energy of the self on the surface of the earth.

Since every individual virtual mind has different past impressions in its memory, no two virtual minds are the same. Therefore, no two fantasy worlds can match each other. This is the reason behind conflicts, wars, crimes, oppressions and restlessness. The virtual mind keeps fantasizing about new things, new tricks, and ways of enjoyment—all operating through ego and generating negative energy. This energy keeps one in a state of doubt, worry, restlessness and stress, giving birth to all negative energies just to sustain itself. It keeps one running, always wanting more and never satisfied.

The moment one stops running and reaches inner peace, they lose the false identity of the 'I', which causes the virtual mind to vanish. As a result, one gets connected to the real and universal mind and finds their real identity of oneness with the universe. The moment one connects with their real identity, they become free of all negative energies, entering a state of everlasting peace and happiness.

∽

A COMPARISON BETWEEN VIRTUAL MIND AND UNIVERSAL MIND

Virtual Mind	Universal Mind
1. Virtual	1. Real
2. Always remains in the past or future	2. Always remains in the present
3. It's in its nature to get distracted	3. It never gets distracted
4. Always divided	4. Always united
6. Has negative energy	6. Has positive energy
7. Belongs to the individual	7. Belongs to the whole universe
8. Contaminated	8. Pure
9. Always under stress	9. Always at peace
10. Full of dualities	10. Non-dual
11. Ever-changing	11. Constant
12. Temporary	12. Permanent
13. Birth and death	13. Eternal
14. Causes severe addiction and suffering	14. Never causes addiction. One remains peaceful.
15. Disconnects one from the source	15. Connects one with the source
16. Wastes the whole energy of the self	16. Remains full of the energy of the self
17. Works as a separate individual	17. Works in harmony with the whole universe
18. Causes suffering all through life	18. Leads to ever-lasting peace and happiness

17

EGO AND ITS MYSTERY

From the moment an innocent child assumes their body as an 'I', they do not know that it will wreak havoc in their life. The resulting illusory 'I' further becomes fascinated by the illusory 'mine', forming an imaginary world of its own. Since this world has separated itself from the real world of oneness, it needs a protector for its survival, which takes the form of the ego. However, this ego is also an illusory protector. As a protector of the tiny illusory world, the ego starts to crave respect and demands regular pampering and praise. It requires high self-respect to preserve its own world, even if it's just a fantasy.

Now let us know its mystery:

1. Ego is an illusion. When an individual witnesses it, it dies as it cannot stand before positive energy of the witness.

2. Ego operates through the virtual mind, which has four functions: deliberation, memory, determination and ego. The conscious mind performs the first three functions, while the subconscious mind performs the fourth (ego) function. However, the subconscious mind is also an illusion. After the third function of determination, the ego strikes one's emotions and feelings like a bullet.

3. Ego will never allow one to find an able teacher. While selecting a teacher, individuals need to satisfy their ego, then select a teacher. However, an ego-less and genuine teacher will not catch one's eye. A story illustrates this point:

   A restless king asked his counsellor if he could introduce him to an able teacher. The counsellor had a person in mind, but the king would not like him. The king insisted, and the counsellor introduced him to his bodyguard. The king took the bodyguard as his teacher and learned that it is not possible to select a genuine and ego-less person through one's own ego.

4. Ego is unpredictable, and so is the egoistic person. One cannot fully rely on an egoistic person as their ego changes with the situation. They may act reliable, but in reality, they may turn out to be the opposite.

5. Ego can team up with others—such as family, community or country—to protect the sense of 'I' and 'mine' in an individual.

Ego is a negative energy that drains energy from an individual and leads them to live in negative energy. Accompanying negative energies include fear, suspicion, restlessness, cleverness, duality, cruelty, sickness, guilt, dishonesty, hatred, ignorance, unfaithfulness, narrow-mindedness, attachment, passion, ugliness, sorrow, dishonour, impurity, foolishness, slavery, discontentment, ruthlessness, irresponsibility, indiscipline, selfishness, anger, greed, jealousy, lust and worry. Ego works tirelessly to protect these negative energies.

Hard work is the ego's language, and negativity is its nature. An ego-less person doesn't need to work hard since they have high levels of self-energy, making work effortless for them. Ironically, people suffering from ego often fail to recognize it, and continue to experience suffering willingly. This leads to the creation of an illusory world. As people become increasingly absorbed in technology, such as pictures, TV, mobile phones, computers, and so on, the problem is getting worse and reducing the life force of the planet or the energy of the self or infinite consciousness. To return to the story:

The king asked his guard teacher about the secret to his happiness. The teacher replied that he was ego-less, and explained how power can corrupt a person and lead them towards egotism. The teacher warned the king about the dangers of making impulsive decisions while under the influence of ego and advised him to wait a few seconds before deciding on things. The teacher told the king to become ego-less and explained how achieving this state would increase the energy of the self.

According to the teacher, ego is like darkness and the energy of the self is like light that illuminates everything. The teacher emphasized that real happiness is not found in material wealth, status, power or physical pleasures, but rather in the Infinite consciousness within us. He taught the king to witness negative emotions, such as anxiety, worries, doubts, and restlessness and to destroy them. The teacher advised the king to accept life with gratitude and connected him to meditation.

The king followed the advice of his teacher and became ego-less, leading him to become a noble king who remained perpetually happy.

18

EMBRACING THE FULLNESS OF THE SELF

Human beings are essentially the energy of the self, and they are most powerful when they are in tune with their true nature. However, people often get trapped in the virtual mind, which impairs their ability to access their full potential. Material energy, which is linked to the virtual mind, obstructs the illumination of the energy of the self.

The movements of one's thoughts, feelings and emotions cloud the energy of the self, thereby decreasing its power. As the distractions increase, the energy becomes weaker, unable to bring about any meaningful change.

However, one can destroy the clouds that form from materialist thinking by connecting to the energy of the Self, resting from within, and increasing their witnessing power. By witnessing the virtual mind, one realizes that they are not the doer; rather, they are the witness. This shift in perspective brings about a sense of power because it aligns one's consciousness with the omnipresent being, which is the witnessing power of the whole universe.

The illusory doer-ship developed by the virtual mind leads to constant distraction, which clouds judgement and moves one away from the energy of the self. The past impressions accumulated in the memory or subconscious mind add to this clouding effect, and this collection grows larger with time. The only way to free oneself from this cycle is to start witnessing the virtual mind and the past impressions or karmas that have accumulated over time.

When a person realizes that they are not the doer but rather the witness, their sense of doer-ship drops automatically. As the power of witnessing grows stronger, the individual comes to the realization that doing is a by-product of the witnessing power. It is like a plant that grows, and bears fruit out of its witnessing power. When a person becomes a witness, everything they do happens spontaneously by itself. Words come out of their mouth, but they do not speak. They walk to distant places, but they never moved. They consume food, but they never eat it. They see everything around them, but they never saw anything. This is the manifestation of witnessing power that expresses itself in doing effortlessly.

As the person continues to witness, they begin to realize

that everything is happening by itself, effortlessly through the power of witnessing. They enter into an unconditional manifestation of their true nature and become connected to the source or infinite consciousness. The energy of the self starts flowing through their body, and they begin to emit positive energy, becoming a source of positive energy themselves. This abolishes all past impressions from their memory. Once these past impressions are cleared, the person becomes a free individual who moves into the ultimate stage of the self, fullness, where they become 'energy of the self' and start to destroy negative energy from their surroundings. If the number of such people increases considerably, the Earth will become free from negative energy, and oneness and harmony will prevail.

As the person becomes the energy of the self, they transcend space and time, I, mine, ego, virtual mind, and the material universe. They become free while living and the ever-changing nature and temporariness of this material universe do not affect them. They remain in everlasting peace and happiness, realizing the non-existence of the egoistic 'I'.

As he continues to witness, the individual realizes that the egoistic 'I' does not exist and that the energy of the self is the only reality that exists in everything and everyone. The person becomes deathless while living, which is the true immortal nature of every human being.

Living in fullness of the self, one sees every being and everything as oneself or a soul. There is no distinction between a cow, a crow, an ant, an elephant, a butcher, or a saint; all are seen alike. One becomes desire-less and goes beyond material gravity. The person remains fully content with whatever they get and wherever they live. They never feel sorrow because they know that the Soul is indestructible. They remain always in ananda, the state of bliss.

Saint Kabir described this stage by saying that it is as if bright light from countless suns had pierced his mind, dispelling every doubt. He added that death instils a dreaded fear into one's mind about feeling ananda, as it is only after attaining it that one can merge with the creator and become the ultimate *ananda swarup*.

19

THE WORLD'S MOST HILARIOUS SURPRISES

As scientific discoveries and technological advancements continue to evolve rapidly, it has taken a toll on the well-being of humanity. While these advancements have provided us with the comforts of labour reduction, faster communication and luxurious living, it has come at a cost—our peace. The addiction to technology and virtual distractions is depleting our energy of the self, leading to a deficiency of positive energy and robbing us of our inner tranquillity. It is surprising to see how people seek solace in religious places and vacations, yet they carry their devices with them, further magnifying the problem.

Our education system, although highly evolved, focuses

on survival skills, overlooking the importance of inner peace. The system has fuelled a competitive mindset, taking a toll on the younger generation's mental, emotional and spiritual well-being. People are draining their energy in running, and our education system fails to emphasize the importance of inner peace. There is a lack of teachings that peace from within is what life and learning should be about. Our system prioritizes efficiency, quality, delivery and service to generate profits, but there is no recognition of the need to recharge one's lost energy of the self.

Ironically, people suffer from the deficiency of energy, which is abundantly available everywhere in the universe. Scientific discoveries, technological advancements, and our education system have pushed people towards a life of constant running, leaving them with no time to recharge and regain their energy of the self.

The universe is an energy of the self that is always at complete rest. When a person is at complete rest, this energy of the self can start filling the void of deficiency. Complete rest means not thinking, feeling, or doing anything. However, due to the addiction of the mind towards distractions, sitting in complete rest without any thoughts, feelings, or actions seems impossible.

The addiction to distraction can only be removed by raising the level of energy of the self through meditation.

A system has been developed for raising the energy of the self at a faster rate. Here is how to do it:

1. Non-doer-ship: Stop becoming a doer and embrace non-doer-ship in your life. The energy of the self that gets wasted in an illusory doer-ship will be saved.
2. Non-ownership: Drop the illusion of ownership. You don't own anything. Whatever is available to you, accept and enjoy it with gratitude.
3. Witnessing thoughts: When you witness your thoughts, negative thoughts disappear. This saves lot of energy.
4. Accept your life as it comes to you with gratitude.
5. Meditation: To reconnect with our souls, we have to cleanse our mind of all impurities so that it comes to rest. Our mind is directly influenced by our breathing. When we are angry, we breathe faster than when we are calm. We can take advantage of this connection between breathing and our state of mind. We can empty our mind temporarily with breathing exercises. When our mind is empty, it comes to rest. This allows us to get easily connected to our soul.

Human beings have seven energy centres. To cleanse the mind properly, we divide them into three parts and exhale with a little force from these places:

a) Between the lowest part of the spine and the navel
b) Between the heart and the navel
c) Slightly above the forehead

This process is to be repeated 40 to 50 times in order of a, b and c. Take the help of an experienced person for this.

By performing this breathing exercise, our mind comes to rest. It gets connected to *anhad shabd* or our soul. Try to listen to the cosmic sound, which various saints have described differently, according to their experiences. Kabir compared it to the sound of the rain. Other saints have compared it variously with the sound of wind, that of beetles, and that of musical instruments like a flute. Now that you are resting in this sound, you can experience your soul, as this sound is the soul. By experiencing it again and again, your connection with the soul is strengthened and your mind is increasingly purified. When the mind is purified, one's connection with the soul is established.

When you remain in meditation for a long time, the path is cleared and you start hearing the sound. This is called *ajapa*. It is the automatic recitation of the sound, also known as auto-recitation. This stage is similar to the stage when you were born.

Guru Nanak openly declared: '*Nam khumari nanka chari rahe din rat*' (I am enjoying the intoxication of the creator's name day and night). Hazrat Mohamad Sahib listened to this sound in a cave for six years. He said, 'I can hear his sound all the time, but your ears are not blessed.' Bodhi Dharma sat facing a wall and listened to the sound for nine years.

The ajapa is a continuous flow of the energy of the self, which is the soul or anhad shabd. It never stops. It destroys all past impressions lying in the subconscious mind and makes one free. After all the past impressions are destroyed, we move into the 'fullness of the self', which is everlasting peace and happiness. It is the blessed stage of ananda.

20

THE ROOT CAUSE OF ALL HUMAN PROBLEMS

Physical comforts have gripped the world. Everything is revolving around the human body. The virtual mind is calling the shots. People are busy trying to satisfy their minds. The mind is an instrument of the body. How one can satisfy an instrument? Human 'I', mine and ego are the offspring of the virtual mind. They have created a virtual world of their own, away from the real world of unconditional manifestation. This fantasy world has pushed people towards a deficiency of energy of the self. Due to this deficiency, humanity is in the grip of problems like:

1. Physical problems
2. Mental problems

3. Suffering from negativity
4. Human relation problems
5. Suffering from greed or the problem of plenty

Along with these problems, the virtual world has pushed humanity into a vicious cycle of past impressions or karmas. Everything one does through doer-ship (virtual mind) goes into one's memory in the form of data. These past impressions are the cause-and-effect of nature. With these karmas, one has moved into the cycle of births and deaths until one is able to come out of the grip of the virtual mind. The root cause of all these problems is the deficiency of energy of the self.

Deficiency in the human system leads to all type of negative energies like fears, doubts, worries, restlessness, anxiety, stress, anger, greed, lust, distrust, lies, dishonesty, narrow mindedness, and so on. These stress the human body organs beyond their limits, resulting in physical sickness, mental sickness and all other problems. An energy-deficient person is like a person sitting in a room. They cannot see the world behind the four walls of their room. Since their self is clouded, the person has no access to any energy of the self. Thus, the person becomes greedy, selfish and narrow-minded. A greedy person has more resources than they can enjoy and even then they keep on chasing more.

We can say that humanity is suffering from a basic sickness of the deficiency of energy of the self. The solution to all human problems lies in raising the level of energy of the self.

A person's superpower is to witness. It is positive energy. If they are able to witness their negative energies, then they can recover from their sickness. Witnessing is the most important exercise to eradicate the greatest enemy of human happiness: negative energy. By practising the superpower of witnessing, a person can effectively observe and detach themselves from the wind of anxiety generated by illusory happiness and sorrow, allowing them to regain inner peace. As a person continues to cultivate this practice and raise their level of energy of the self, they can transcend the grip of their virtual mind.

At higher levels of energy, the virtual mind disappears— along with the sense of 'I', mine and ego—leading to a state of oneness and harmony with the universe. In this stage, the superpower of the self works in synchronization with the human body, allowing one to enjoy life in a way that cannot be described in human words.

21

WHY CAN'T WE
WALK ON THE SIMPLE PATH?

The physical world is the known world, and we have full experience of living in this world. The real world, however, is unknown. We do not have any experience of it. When an individual starts moving on this path by connecting to the source, their energy level begins to rise and control is gained over the mind. The addicted mind starts feeling uncomfortable, causing anxiety. Why then do we want to do it? This anxiety gives rise to so many doubts. Such doubts further give rise to the fear of the unknown. So, people do not want to leave the known realm and enter this unknown world.

There are two main hurdles:

1. Individual ego
2. Lack of faith

INDIVIDUAL EGO

Each individual takes decisions after convincing their ego. For a decision to travel an unknown path, it is very difficult to convince the ego for two reasons. Firstly, it is unknown, and secondly, it is to eradicate ego itself. So, it is nearly impossible to convince the ego.

LACK OF FAITH

All human powers lie in the energy of the self. A person with low level of energy of the self will have less faith, which will restrict their journey on this path. For these reasons, most religions have given high importance to congregations to tread this path. It is to take advantage of the collective energy of the self to take care of individual ego as well as to strengthen the faith of each individual.

For an individual, there is nothing to be done as they are not a doer. Things are only to be understood. If they understand how they have fallen into the illusory world of suffering from the real world, they will automatically start moving in the right direction. Many people are conditioned to believe that constant doing is the way to achieve success and happiness. However, it is only through understanding that a person can truly overcome suffering and find lasting contentment. By cultivating this awareness, a person's energy of the self will begin to rise, and they will be able to visualize that things are happening by themselves.

As they progress on this path, their faith will be strengthened, and the journey will become easier. Eventually, they will reach their destination, which is the real world of oneness and harmony with the universe.

The metaphor of a kite being lifted by the wind, a spinner on a twisted thread, and impure gold being melted and purified—all illustrate the idea that things must go through a process of motion and transformation before coming to rest. Similarly, negative emotions such as anxiety, doubt and fear can drive the mind to continue running. But once these illusions are released, the mind will come to rest, and the person will enter the real world of oneness.

ਰਾਮਾਨੰਦ ਜੀ ਘਰ-੧ ੴ ਸਤਿਗੁਰ ਪ੍ਰਸਾਦਿ ॥

ਕਤ ਜਾਈਐ ਰੇ ਘਰ ਲਾਗੋ ਰੰਗੁ ॥

ਮੇਰਾ ਚਿਤੁ ਨਾ ਚਲੈ ਮਨੁ ਭਇਓ ਪੰਗੁ ॥੧॥ ਰਹਾਉ ॥

ਏਕ ਦਿਵਸ ਮਨ ਭਈ ਉਮੰਗ ॥

ਘਸਿ ਚੰਦਨ ਚੋਆ ਬਹੁ ਸੁਗੰਧ ॥

ਪੂਜਨ ਚਾਲੀ ਬ੍ਰਹਮ ਠਾਇ ॥

ਸੋ ਬ੍ਰਹਮ ਬਤਾਇਓ ਗੁਰ ਮਨ ਹੀ ਮਾਹਿ ॥੧॥

ਜਹਾ ਜਾਈਐ ਤਹ ਜਲ ਪਖਾਨ ॥

ਤੂ ਪੂਰਿ ਰਹਿਓ ਹੈ ਸਭ ਸਮਾਨ ॥

ਬੇਦ ਪੁਰਾਨ ਸਭ ਦੇਖੇ ਜੋਇ ॥

ਊਹਾਂ ਤਉ ਜਾਈਐ ਜਉ ਈਹਾਂ ਨ ਹੋਇ ॥੨॥

ਸਤਿਗੁਰ ਮੈ ਬਲਿਹਾਰੀ ਤੋਰ ॥

ਜਿਨਿ ਸਕਲ ਬਿਕਲ ਭ੍ਰਮ ਕਾਟੇ ਮੋਰ ॥

ਰਾਮਾਨੰਦ ਸੁਆਮੀ ਰਮਤ ਬ੍ਰਹਮ ॥

ਗੁਰ ਕਾ ਸਬਦੁ ਕਾਟੈ ਕੋਟਿ ਕਰਮ ॥੩॥

Meaning of Shabd Shri Rama Nand:

Where are you going when celebrations are going on in your inner being? My energy cannot flow freely as my mind is obstructing it time and again. One day, a deep desire swelled in my mind to make preparations to go to the Creator's place to worship him. But then I remembered that my guru told me that the Creator resides in the mind itself. Wherever we go, there is water and garbage. The Creator is present in everything alike. Who dispels all his doubts thanks the Creator. He remains merged with the Creator and declares that anhad shabd (energy of the self) destroys crores of past impressions or karmas (to free a person from the material world).

ਸ਼ਬਦ ਸ੍ਰੀ ਨਾਮਦੇਓ

ਆਨੀਲੇ ਕਾਗਦੁ ਕਾਟੀਲੇ ਗੁਡੀ ਆਕਾਸ ਮਧੇ ਭਰਮੀਅਲੇ ॥

ਪੰਚ ਜਨਾ ਸਿਉ ਬਾਤ ਬਤਉਆ ਚੀਤੁ ਸੁ ਡੋਰੀ ਰਾਖੀਅਲੇ ॥ 1 ॥

ਮਨੁ ਰਾਮ ਨਾਮਾ ਬੇਧੀਅਲੇ ॥

ਜੈਸੇ ਕਨਿਕ ਕਲਾ ਚਿਤੁ ਮਾਂਡੀਅਲੇ ॥ 1 ॥ ਰਹਾਉ॥

ਆਨੀਲੇ ਕੁੰਭ ਭਰਾਈਲੇ ਉਦਕ ਰਾਜ ਕੁਆਰਿ ਪੁਰੰਦਰੀਏ ॥
ਹਸਤ ਬਿਨੋਦ ਬੀਚਾਰ ਕਰਤੀ ਹੈ ਚੀਤੁ ਸੁ ਗਾਗਰਿ ਰਾਖੀਅਲੇ ॥ 2 ॥

ਮੰਦਰੁ ਏਕੁ ਦੁਆਰ ਦਸ ਜਾ ਕੇ ਗਊ ਚਰਾਵਨ ਛਾਡੀਅਲੇ ॥

ਪਾਂਚ ਕੋਸ ਪਰ ਗਊ ਚਰਾਵਤ ਚੀਤੁ ਸੁ ਬਛਰਾ ਰਾਖੀਅਲੇ ॥ 3 ॥

ਕਹਤ ਨਾਮਦੇਉ ਸੁਨਹੁ ਤਿਲੋਚਨ ਬਾਲਕੁ ਪਾਲਨ ਪਉਢੀਅਲੇ ॥

ਅੰਤਰਿ ਬਾਹਰਿ ਕਾਜ ਬਿਰੁਧੀ ਚੀਤੁ ਸੁ ਬਾਲਕੁ ਰਾਖੀਅਲੇ

॥ 4 ॥ 1 ॥ 972 ॥

The great Saint Namdev explains real-life experiences to his friend, Tilochan:

He says: Just as a person flying a kite keeps witnessing the string of the kite while talking to his friends. Just as young girls walking back to their homes after fetching water from the well keep witnessing their pitchers filled with water on their heads while laughing, gossiping and conversing. Just as a cow keeps witnessing its newborn calf while grazing in a field miles away; just as the mother of a little child keeps witnessing the child while doing household chores inside and outside the house; in the same way, a person on the stage (free from the material world) witnesses himself while leading a normal, materialistic life. He is always in ananda.

To be born as a human being is nature's most precious gift. Life lived in everlasting peace and happiness transcends itself in the end.

22

SPACETIME AND BEYOND

According to science, electromagnetism and gravity make up the three dimensions of space, namely length, width and height. The fourth dimension is time, the order of events. Therefore, 'spacetime' is one thing, like two faces of the same coin.

The interaction between electromagnetism and gravity gave birth to matter energy followed by time. So, this universe which we see with our physical eyes is the product of 'spacetime'. Therefore, this falls under the control of spacetime. Spacetime is nature which works in this universe powered by the infinite consciousness, which is energy of the self or soul. Since space emerges from the infinite consciousness, it falls under the control of the infinite consciousness, self or soul. Therefore, ultimate control over spacetime or nature or matter belongs to the infinite consciousness.

The infinite consciousness, self or soul is the ultimate power for giving birth to this material universe, running this universe, and taking back to its fold in the end. There is only one ultimate power responsible for everything and every being and that is the infinite consciousness. People call it by various names throughout the world. When a person gets connected to this ultimate power of the infinite consciousness, self or soul, they go beyond spacetime.

Spacetime: Space is present in each and every particle of the universe. Since particles are always in motion; space keeps on changing everywhere and every time. With this change of spacetime, everything and every being is changing at every moment. Therefore, change is the nature of this universe. Because of this change, there is impermanence in the whole material universe. It cannot always stay the way it is. At a certain age, everything and every being that has come into existence will have to return to the formless, which is the infinite consciousness.

Spacetime is constantly changing, causing everything and every being to change as well. Our main problem is that we are unable to see this change and mistakenly view things and beings as permanent. This causes us to cling to them and suffer when they inevitably change or die. However, we can never control spacetime or space itself, as even when we are at rest there is change happening within us. Digestion and blood flow are just a few examples.

When it comes to time, it is merely a name for change itself. Therefore, the only option is to accept and understand this natural phenomenon of change at its roots. When we do this, our clinging to things and beings starts to recede. We feel free, and the energy of the self that was once wasted in clinging is saved. This brings relief and allows us to regain the energy of the self.

∽

THE PROBLEM OF QUITTING

We often cling to things and beings, hoping for permanence and becoming addicted to them. When they eventually change or die, it causes us great disturbance and suffering because we never expected such an outcome. We become hurt and depressed, realizing that we suffer because of our attachment to things and beings.

In our attempt to alleviate this suffering, we may try to escape from these things and beings and find a peaceful place away from them. However, we fail to recognize that they are not separate from us but reside within our minds as addiction to past impressions in our memory. Wherever we go, they will follow us. We cannot escape this suffering by simply leaving them behind.

Eventually, we come to the realization that quitting is not the solution. The only option left is to tread the middle path—

that is, neither clinging nor quitting—and find balance and acceptance in the natural phenomenon of change.

ℒ

THE SOLUTION IS THE MIDDLE PATH

The solution to our problem is not in clinging or quitting, but in accepting life as it is. When we do so, the changes of space and time become acceptable to us, and we transcend space and time to arrive at a state of rest. As Guru Nanak and Buddha have said, accepting the will of the universe and witnessing the waves of the ocean without getting involved with them can take us beyond space and time.

According to Ashtavakra, many people do not realize that their efforts can bring sorrow. However, a person who deeply understands this fact is a man of true knowledge and can go beyond suffering. Being content, having free senses and staying connected to the self leads to the fullness of the self. Within the fullness of the self, one becomes the energy of the self itself.

Just as a flower in a remote place spreads its beauty and fragrance without needing anyone to notice it, a person living in the fullness of the self spreads positive energy around without worrying about recognition. Living beyond space and time, one can solve all their problems and enjoy everlasting peace and happiness.

The observer of the universe is the Absolute Being:

Brahman (also known as infinite consciousness, self or soul). As human beings are also the self or soul, their basic power is to witness. When a person lives in the fullness of the self, they become a true witness, and their illusory world vanishes automatically. Negative thoughts and energies like fear, worries, anxiety, restlessness and doubts dissipate in the face of the witnessing power. This witnessing self rests beyond space and time in absolute peace and ananda (bliss).

PART-3

LIFE: A CELEBRATION

This universe (the Absolute Being) is positive energy and at complete rest, that is, in ananda. It is present in each and every particle of its creation in the form of vibrations of positive energy. When this universe is full of positive energy, how can there be any sorrow?

There is no sorrow anywhere. Human beings are an exception. Thanks to the ego, there is human greed, which blocks the mind from receiving vibrations, leading to a deficiency of positive energy.

A person of knowledge who has deeply realized this fact, abandons their greed and accepts life as it is. They start receiving these vibrations and get filled with positive energy. Then they are able to move into their true nature of everlasting peace and happiness, which is ananda.

Ananda is a stage when you realize that you are nothing but self or soul, which is the universe. You further realize that this body is a miraculous gift of nature through which you have come to watch the celebrations of this physical world.

23

THE POWER TO WITNESS
IS A MIRACLE

The heart centre is the centre of all the seven centres in the human body. It is located in the heart. It is the centre of feeling, love, compassion and detached universal love. Kaivaly Upanishad says that meditating on the lotus of your heart in the centre is the most untainted, exquisitely pure, clear and sorrowless of infinite forms.

Sage Vashishta told Rama, 'In the peace of one's own inner being, consciousness vibrates and world vision arises. If this consciousness does not vibrate there would be no world vision. This vibration of consciousness is the cosmic sound or anhad shabd.'

The inner being is the place where lies the ocean of ananda. It is the place where there is no change. It is beyond space

Human Heart Centre

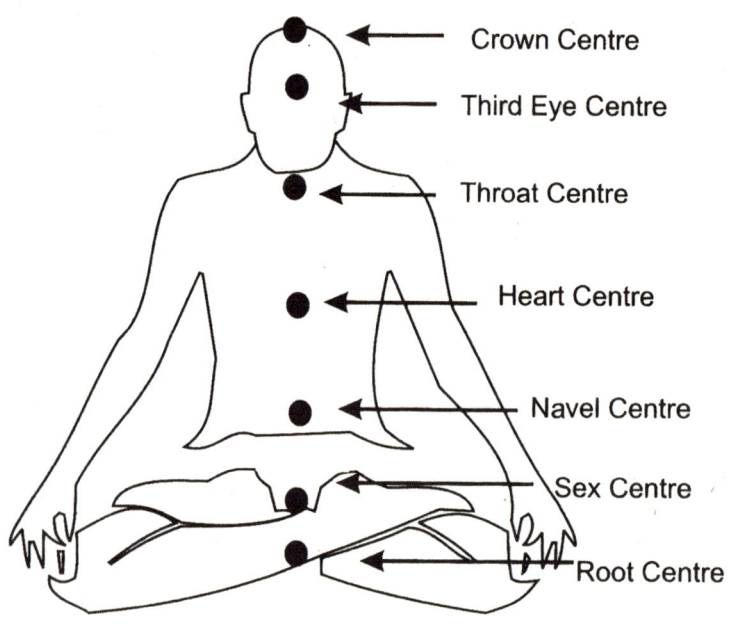

Crown Centre

Third Eye Centre

Throat Centre

Heart Centre

Navel Centre

Sex Centre

Root Centre

and time. It is the place where mind does not begin. It is the place where material gravity does not prevail. This is the most pious place in the body where you can be one with yourself and the universe.

You were never separated from this universe. Material gravity gave you a feeling that you are separate from the universe and belong to Earth. Gurus have always instructed us to connect to the place from where the journey of earthly life began. Upon connecting, we come to know that life is just a projection of gravity passing over ourselves. In reality there is no birth and no death. Whenever you are in the grip of bad thoughts or negative energy, witnessing them through your heart centre, which is the place of their origin, is the solution.

Guru Nanak in his Gurbani Japji Sahib said:

'*Suniye, maniye, man kita bhao, antar gat theerath mal nhao.*' This means, 'Listen to the anhad shabad, believe him, and fall in love with him. This is happening in your inner being, which is the holy centre of pilgrimage. Meditate on the same.'

The fifth guru, Shri Guru Arjan Dev, established the Golden Temple complex in Amritsar on the basis of the human body to enlighten people that the body is the real temple for the Creator, and the Creator of the universe is present in the body at all times. If you connect to this place, you will go beyond suffering. He built the Golden Temple in the holy pond at the place which can be correlated with the heart centre of the human body to make people understand that anhad shabd or cosmic vibrations are happening all the time in the body, just like the sacred *gurbani* is being recited in the Golden Temple all the time.

He said in his Gurbani, '*Antar guru aradhana, jehva jap guru nao, netri nat nuru pekhna, sarvani sunna gurnao, satguru sati ratia, dargah paiye thaon, kaho nanak kirpa kare jisno eh vathdeh, jag mein utam kadiye, virle keyie kay.*'

Shri Guru Arjan Dev has described the ultimate stage of how to remain in the fullness of the self. He says that when auto recitation (ajapa) is going on in your inner being, keep reciting His name with your tongue. What you witness is Him and what you hear is also Him. This way you are easily absorbed in yourself and become free while living.

Guru says, 'This can happen when He blesses a person. Very few have received such grace in this universe. Shri Guru Teg Bahadur, the ninth Sikh guru, in his Gurbani, said, '*Ram nam ur main gahio jake sum nahi koye, jis simrat sankat mite daras tuharo hoye.*'

This means meditating on your inner being is the ultimate form of meditation. By doing this, suffering vanishes and one meets the Creator of the universe. Human self, soul, attention or awareness contain all the treasures one is seeking. Wisdom, health, material wealth, desire fulfilment, freedom, peace of mind and everlasting happiness are not in the body. So, in order to lead a life of everlasting peace and happiness, one needs to raise the level of the energy of the self and witness one's thoughts, negativity and the virtual mind.

COMING OUT OF RESTLESSNESS

Our restless state of mind, which is born out of the ego, is the primary reason for our suffering. However, if we can understand the nature of our virtual or false mind, we can free ourselves from its grip. The virtual mind can be compared to darkness, which is not an actual entity or thing but instead a lack of light. Similarly, the false mind is not a tangible thing, but rather a lack of energy from the self. To overcome the grip of the false mind, we must focus on the energy of the self rather than directly trying to deal with the false mind. For instance, when we experience restlessness, we can bring in attention and witness our restlessness at our heart centre. This is like bringing light into darkness and the same goes for the restlessness that our virtual mind creates. Witnessing our restlessness or sorrows helps us come out of them, and we suffer as long as we remain unaware of them.

It is surprising to see that people who are made of positive energy themselves can suffer from negativity or a deficiency of positive energy due to ignorance. A person of knowledge understands that the virtual mind creates all negative energies, such as fear, worry, restlessness, doubt and stress. By remaining a witness to the virtual mind, one can keep negative energy out of their life and enjoy everlasting happiness. Developing the habit of being a witness to our thoughts can solve most of the problems in our lives.

Our virtual mind is never in the present. It always hops

between the past and the future. However, life happens in the present moment. We are always happy when we live in the present. In the present moment, there is no virtual mind. Therefore, we must remain mindful and witness our virtual mind for its new demands and cravings. The virtual mind keeps dragging us towards new temptations and doubts to keep us on the run because it survives by keeping us busy with unnecessary things. People who obey their virtual mind can never be happy or satisfied because the false mind can never feel fulfilled. It only exists in our imagination and is not real.

Our witnessing power is a miracle and can help tame our virtual mind. Our virtual mind cannot stay before our witness, just as darkness cannot exist before light. Witnessing our virtual mind will help us stay happy and peaceful.

24

THE UNIVERSE AS UNCONDITIONAL MANIFESTATION

The universe, soul, self and infinite consciousness (The Absolute Being) is present in every being and everything. He has space as His body and a universal mind. He vibrates in each and every particle of the universe. He sees through all eyes, hears through all ears, works through all hands, tastes through all tongues, walks through all feet, thinks through all brains, feels through all hearts, and memorizes through all memories. He is the one who is running the universe but remains a silent spectator and does not involve himself anywhere. He is present at all times and holds all memories. He alone is present in space, which keeps His energy, but He remains beyond space and time. This is how it is unconditional manifestation.

This is how He is the reason behind every situation, happening, thought, emotion, feeling, perception—and their effects—but remains uninvolved as a salient spectator, observer or witness. He is effortless, ananda or everlasting happiness.

25

TRUE HUMAN LIFE IS ANANDA

The universe is a single organism, and everything is interdependent. This means that we are in everything, and everything is in us. The universe is ananda or effortless since its inception, and as human beings, we are also ananda. However, out of ignorance, we have developed a great misunderstanding by thinking of our bodies as 'I am' instead of the self or soul. This false 'I am' separates us from the universe and pushes us into the illusory world of ego, mine and the illusory mind. This blocks us from receiving positive vibrations from the universe and pushes us into a negative energy cycle of suffering.

To become one with the universe again, we need to drop the false 'I am' and reach all the attributes of 'One'. We need not do anything to be happy because it is our basic nature.

We simply need to be ourselves, be always effortless in doing everything, and always be at rest from within.

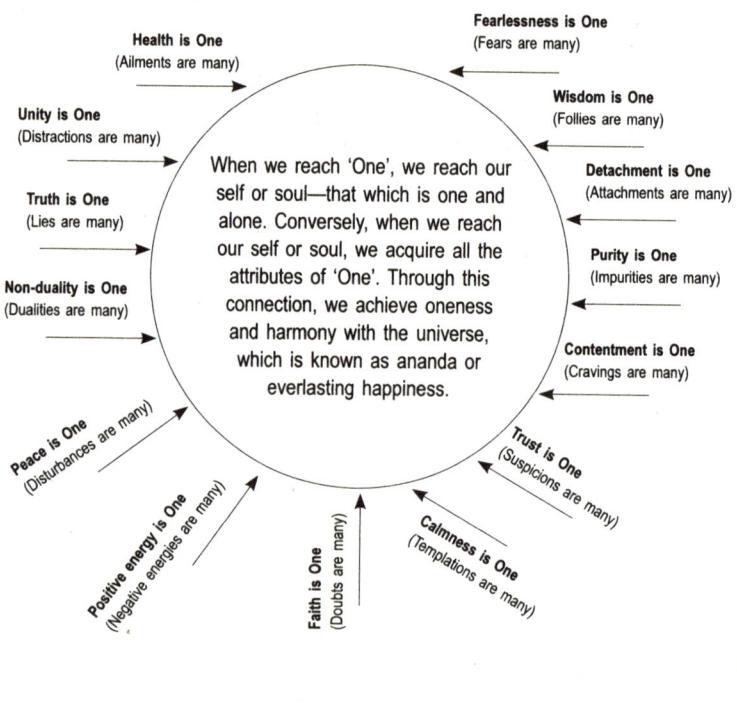

True Human Life is Ananda
(Happiness is one but sorrows are many)

Fearlessness is One
(Fears are many)

Health is One
(Ailments are many)

Unity is One
(Distractions are many)

Wisdom is One
(Follies are many)

Truth is One
(Lies are many)

Detachment is One
(Attachments are many)

Non-duality is One
(Dualities are many)

Purity is One
(Impurities are many)

Contentment is One
(Cravings are many)

When we reach 'One', we reach our self or soul—that which is one and alone. Conversely, when we reach our self or soul, we acquire all the attributes of 'One'. Through this connection, we achieve oneness and harmony with the universe, which is known as ananda or everlasting happiness.

Peace is One
(Disturbances are many)

Positive energy is One
(Negative energies are many)

Faith is One
(Doubts are many)

Calmness is One
(Temptations are many)

Trust is One
(Suspicions are many)

THE IGNORANCE OF HUMANS

Humanity is suffering from a funny kind of ignorance. We are deficient in the positive energy that the universe is made of.

This energy is in abundance everywhere. This positive energy contains all the treasures and powers that we seek, including peace and everlasting happiness. Yet, we waste this energy day and night in ignorance by running after petty objects and pleasures, which we could easily obtain by staying at peace and at rest with our selves.

26

THE YOUNG BOY AND THE SAINT

A young boy went to a saint for advice on how to be happy in his marriage while living with his parents. He showed the saint a picture of the beautiful girl he wanted to marry, and expressed his concerns. The saint smiled and responded, 'Do not forget that this girl is coming with past impressions or karmas in her memory. Imagine that everyone has ten bags full of past impressions, including your wife, parents, and future children—that makes 60 bags of past impressions in your home. These past impressions do not always correspond with each other, as they heavily influence people's lives. So, how can a person be happy in a shared space with 60 bags full of negative energy from six different people?'

Upon hearing this, the boy became frightened and asked

the saint if there was a solution. The saint reassured him that there is a solution to every problem. He explained that these 60 bags of past impressions are nothing more than a delusion, and not real. They are like clouds of subtle material that overshadow the energy of the self and restrict its illumination. This often leads to negative consequences such as powerlessness and misery. The self continually interprets these clouds into distinct shapes and forms through thoughts, feelings, emotions, doubts and dreams, which are all negative energies. This negative energy can easily destroy family harmony. But this is just like darkness that can be overcome by lighting a lamp.

The saint suggested that one can overcome the negative energy of 60 bags by connecting with their self (soul) through meditation. This is a positive energy that is self-illuminating. When one meditates as a group in their family, there is a greater chance of dissolving negative clouds from past events and preventing unsettled arguments or conflicts from arising. Through meditation, one can connect with the universe and become one with it.

The saint explained that wherever people meditate, positive energy fills the space, bringing peace and harmony. He went on to say that the universe is a play of awareness and that the level of our awareness directly affects our happiness; the lower the awareness, the less happiness we experience. To experience everlasting happiness, we must raise our awareness by shedding our ego, observing our thoughts, accepting our life as it is, and meditating. Our virtual mind creates an illusion of pleasure by constantly seeking instant gratification through the senses, but this gives only temporary satisfaction. True happiness comes from connecting with our real self, which is the source of everything in the universe, including everlasting peace and happiness.

The main problem with humans, the saint explained, is that they tend to forget their real self and prioritize survival through education and memorization. However, our life and happiness depend on our self or soul, which lies within our intentions. When we have good intentions, our energy rises, making us powerful and happy, and conversely, bad intentions cause stress and decrease our energy, making us powerless and miserable.

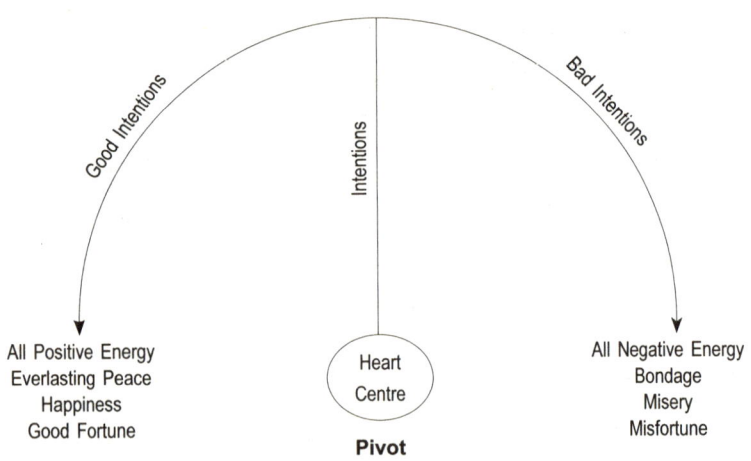

The addictiveness of the virtual mind obscures the truth and causes feelings of insecurity, leading individuals to drain their self of energy and causing suffering and conflict. Shri Krishna explains in the Bhagavad Gita that our self is both our friend and enemy: obeying it results in harmony with the universe, while disobeying it creates conflict. Witnessing our intentions is the first step towards experiencing everlasting peace and happiness.

To enjoy a prosperous, healthy and harmonious life, people should have good intentions and meditate daily. Seeking pleasure through the five senses leads to addiction and perpetual chasing of low-awareness sense pleasures. However, a person with higher awareness realizes the worthlessness of sense pleasures, experiences them fully, and settles for ananda from the energy of the self.

It's surprising that people often don't realize that the universe resides within them instead of outside. Thinking that the universe is external, they try to improve it, which is impossible because it's beyond their control. However, when a person of knowledge improves themselves and settles into their true nature, the outside universe automatically starts settling around them.

Human life in the material world is based on one's past impressions, which are invisible. Thus, it's hard to know someone's true nature just by interacting or seeing them. It takes time to get to know someone. As these past impressions differ for each person, so do their behaviour and destiny. When humans connect with their self or soul, they go beyond their past impressions and come in harmony and oneness with the universe. This compatibility continuously increases, which is essential for daily living or working together.

Human life is a play of perception that changes with the type of energy one possesses. When a person is filled with positive energy, they become a good person and their behaviour changes accordingly. They are in harmony with those around them. When their level of positive energy decreases, they become selfish, introverted, greedy and egoistic. They spread negative energy in the environment. The solution lies in connecting everyone with their energy of the self. After this connection, every person improves.

Life is inherently simple, but our tendency to complicate it makes it harder to see the positive energy that surrounds us. This energy is invisible, and many people don't even realize that it's their own energy of the self, which is a superpower. However, this energy can be accessed through simple means. The main obstacle to receiving this energy is our 'I' and ego, which creates restlessness and hinders our ability to come to rest and access positive energy. Once we come to rest from within, this energy begins to fill the deficiency in us, which positively impacts our behaviour towards others.

It's interesting how people have invented various ways to escape their 'I' or ego and find rest, such as drinking intoxicants, taking drugs, watching movies, listening to music, going to nightclubs or reading books. However, these are just temporary solutions that don't let them experience a deep and lasting sense of rest. If people manage to sit idle for some time each day, they can receive positive energy wherever they are.

People can also create a happy atmosphere at home and work, which helps them receive positive energy continuously. For instance, when they laugh, they receive this energy in abundance because they let go of their 'I' and ego and come to complete rest. Helping others is another way to receive positive energy because while doing so, their 'I' and ego disappear, and they become connected to the oneness of the universe.

Living a simple and ego-less life is essential for receiving the superpower—the energy of the self or positive energy from one's surroundings. Such positive energy, when present in abundance, can turn Earth into heaven. Therefore, even a small increase in positive energy on the planet can have a tremendous impact, just as a small candle lit in a dark hall can suddenly make everything visible.

27

THE HOLY UNIVERSE IS A PLACE OF CELEBRATION

The universe is fundamentally made up of positive energy. It's the source of everything that exists, sustains everything that exists, and eventually takes everything back into its fold. When a person accumulates an abundance of positive energy, they become wonderstruck by the miracles that happen all around them. They see positive energy dancing in every living being—from plants, birds and animals to the sun, moon, planets, galaxies, rivers, fertile lands, deserts and mountains.

People who experience an abundance of positive energy get overwhelmed by its presence in their own body. They also feel pained to see how many others are bereft of it. They witness the beauty, perfection, diversity, flexibility, compatibility and self-sufficiency of positive energy, where words of any language fall short of describing its mesmerizing impact. They see celebrations of life happening everywhere, and this fills them with joy and gratitude.

EPILOGUE

This is an enlightening story about the great rishi, Vedvyas, who is known for writing the Vedas, and his son, Sukhdev. Sukhdev had learned all the Vedas and become an egoistic person, believing that he was the most learned man. He then renounced his worldly possessions and started living an austere life, wearing only a small piece of cloth called 'langoti'. This, in turn, added to his ego, and he became popular with the masses as Sukhdev Muni, the most egoistic and angry young man. Though his father tried to help him, all his efforts were in vain.

One day, Sukhdev went to his father and told him that, despite having all his knowledge and renouncing worldly pleasures, he was miserable and didn't know what to do. His father advised him to go to King Janak and accept him as his teacher. Sukhdev reluctantly followed his father's advice and proceeded towards King Janak's palace on foot. On the way, he kept thinking about how a king living in a magnificent palace, leading a luxurious life, could become the teacher of such a learned and austere man like him. He imagined the king sitting on a golden chair among his counsellors, watching young ladies dance, taking intoxicants, and enjoying a sumptuous meal while laughing and gossiping in the palace hall at night. Sukhdev kept cursing his father, thinking that the old man's discrimination power had faded and he had sent him to the wrong person.

After a long journey, Sukhdev reached King Janak's palace and saw the same scene that he had fantasized about on his way. This further convinced him that his father had sent him to the wrong place. One of the guards received him and informed the king that the son of the great rishi Vedvyas wanted to see him outside. The king greeted Sukhdev Muni with respect, touching his feet and washing them with his own hands before asking him to rest and eat.

According to the routine, the king woke Sukhdev in the morning and invited him to bathe in a nearby river with him. During the bath, Sukhdev suddenly started crying loudly, claiming that the king's palace was burning. The king calmly reassured him that it was not his palace and that the people working there would take care of it. However, Sukhdev persisted in his delusion, crying out, 'Hai meri langoti, hai meri langoti,' and ran back to his room to find it and his langoti safe. He returned to the king, relieved, but the king laughed and told him that he had failed his first lesson. Thus, King Janak began to teach Sukhdev.

FIRST LESSON

King Janak's first lesson to Sukhdev was about detachment and clinging. He explained that his palace and lavish lifestyle did not define him, as he remained detached from them. Sukhdev, on the other hand, had renounced everything and embraced a simple life but was still clinging to his langoti. King Janak emphasized that true renunciation does not lie in giving up material things but in the absence of attachment. He advised Sukhdev to enjoy things without clinging and with gratitude to achieve inner peace.

SECOND LESSON

In the second lesson, the king pointed out that Sukhdev may have gained knowledge from the Vedas, but he had not yet connected to himself. He emphasized that true learning meant connecting with oneself. Through meditation, King Janak helped Sukhdev achieve self-realization and realize that the self is what gives birth, runs, and takes back everything and everyone in the universe.

Sukhdev became thankful to King Janak for his teachings and began to practise them. He realized that his father sending him to such a great teacher was the right decision.

THIRD LESSON

The third lesson imparted by King Janak to Sukhdev was about the importance of self-awareness in navigating the material world. He asked Sukhdev to come to him in the evening when the earthen lamps filled with oil and a wick inside, called 'diya', were traditionally lit. He placed a lighted lamp on Sukhdev's palm and instructed him to go and see the palace from within, warning him to take care not to let the lamp burn off, or he would be stuck inside.

Sukhdev went into the palace with the lighted lamp and returned after a long time, still holding the lamp in his palm. When Janak asked him about the palace, Sukhdev replied that he could not see it, as his focus was entirely on safeguarding the lighted lamp from burning off.

Janak used the metaphor of the lighted lamp to illustrate the nature of the material world. He explained that one could easily get stuck in the cycle of birth and rebirth if they let the light of their self-awareness go off. Therefore, it is essential to keep the lamp of self-awareness always lit while enjoying and experiencing the world.

FOURTH LESSON

The fourth lesson taught by King Janak is about letting go of the ego and accepting everything that comes our way with grace and equanimity. He tested Sukhdev's progress in this regard by asking him to stand in a pit and getting thousands of *pattals*, covered with leftover food, thrown on his head by the sadhus who attended the free lunch.

Despite being drenched in leftover food, Sukhdev showed no signs of anger or remorse. Rather, he had accepted the incident with a heart full of peace and tranquillity. King Janak embraced him, congratulating him on his success, and reinforced the teachings that self-awareness and detachment lead to the dissolution of the ego and the transformation of the material universe into a place of celebration.

GLOSSARY

1. **Advaita**: Non-dual or unique
2. **Ajapa**: Continuous auto-recitation or continuous, endless meditation
3. **Amrit**: The nectar that gives you eternal life
4. **Ananda**: Eternal bliss, a stage beyond joy and sorrow, a stage of complete rest from within, or a condition of full development from within
5. **Ananda swarup:** Eternal peace or bliss
6. **Anhad shabd**: An automatic and non-instrumental sound that is unending and knows no limits; the voice of silence; the cosmic sound; the vibration of the infinite consciousness.
7. **Atma**: Soul, self, or the infinite consciousness
8. **Bhagavad Gita**: One of the holy books of Hinduism. It contains teachings that are said to have come from Lord Krishna. The Gita is a doctrine of universal truth.

9. **Dhyaan:** Infinite consciousness or self or soul or awareness
10. **Ganga:** A holy river
11. **Karma:** Cause and effect or impressions lying in the subconscious mind
12. **Mala:** A string of beads used for praying
13. **Parvati:** Nature or the material world or that which is relative
14. **Sansa:** False
15. **Sansar:** The material world or the restlessness of human beings
16. **Sehaj:** Eternal peace or eternal joy
17. **Sehaj samadhi:** Effortless meditation
18. **Shiva:** Infinite consciousness or universal soul or the absolute
19. **Sukham:** Inner peace or inner joy
20. **Pattal:** Tree Leaf used as a plate to eat food